ANIMALS OF
AFRICA & EUROPE

ANIMALS OF AFRICA & EUROPE

A VISUAL ENCYCLOPEDIA OF AMPHIBIANS, REPTILES AND MAMMALS IN THE AFRICAN
AND EUROPEAN CONTINENTS, WITH OVER 350 ILLUSTRATIONS AND PHOTOGRAPHS

TOM JACKSON

CONSULTANT: MICHAEL CHINERY

southwater

This edition is published by Southwater

Southwater is an imprint of Anness Publishing Ltd
Hermes House, 88–89 Blackfriars Road, London SE1 8HA
tel. 020 7401 2077; fax 020 7633 9499
www.southwaterbooks.com; info@anness.com

© Anness Publishing Ltd 2004

UK agent: The Manning Partnership Ltd,
tel. 01225 478444; fax 01225 478440; sales@manning-partnership.co.uk
UK distributor: Grantham Book Services Ltd,
tel. 01476 541080; fax 01476 541061; orders@gbs.tbs-ltd.co.uk
North American agent/distributor: National Book Network,
tel. 301 459 3366; fax 301 429 5746; www.nbnbooks.com
Australian agent/distributor: Pan Macmillan Australia,
tel. 1300 135 113; fax 1300 135 103; customer.service@macmillan.com.au
New Zealand agent/distributor: David Bateman Ltd, tel. (09) 415 7664; fax (09) 415 8892

A CIP catalogue record for this book is available from the British Library.

Publisher: Joanna Lorenz
Editorial Director: Judith Simons
Project Editor: Felicity Forster
Copy Editors: Gerard Cheshire, Richard Rosenfeld
and Jen Green
Illustrators: Stuart Carter, Jim Channell, John Francis,
Stephen Lings, Alan Male, Shane Marsh and Sarah Smith
Map Illustrator: Anthony Duke
Designer: Nigel Partridge
Production Controller: Claire Rae

Illustrations appearing on pages 1–5: page 1 ruffed lemur; page 2 giraffes; page 3 lions;
page 4t hippopotamus; page 4b vervet; page 5 (top row, from left to right) aardwolf, baboons,
rhinoceros; page 5 (bottom row, from left to right) lioness, bat-eared fox, cheetah

Previously published as part of a larger volume,
The World Encyclopedia of Animals

1 3 5 7 9 10 8 6 4 2

CONTENTS

UNDERSTANDING ANIMALS

This book examines amphibians, reptiles and mammals of Africa and Europe, but can only scratch the surface of the fantastic range of life forms packed on these continents. It concentrates on the vertebrates (the group of animals that have a backbone, which includes the above three groups as well as birds and fish); however, vertebrates form just one of the 31 major animal groups. The huge diversity of life contained in the other groups cannot rival the most familiar vertebrates for size, strength or general popularity. For most people, slugs are not in the same league as tigers, nor can crickets and crabs compete with dolphins and lions. Yet these relatively unpopular animals are capable of amazing feats. For example, squid travel by jet propulsion, mussels change sex as they get older, and ants live in harmony in colonies of millions.

The diversity of life among the vertebrates is mind-boggling. A blue whale is 30m (100ft) long, while the smallest salamander is less than 3cm (1¼in) long. The rest appear in every shape and size in between. Yet vertebrates are not distinguished by their bodies alone but by the unusual ways in which they use them. For example, a lizard will shed its tail if a hungry predator clamps its jaws around it, and while the tail-less reptile escapes, its attacker is kept occupied by the still-wriggling appendage. And hunting bats, which can fly thanks to the skin stretched over their elongated hand bones, so creating wings, manage to locate their prey in the dark by using sonar. They bark out high-pitched calls that bounce off surrounding objects, and the time taken for the echo to return signifies the size and location of whatever is out there. These are just three examples of the extraordinary diversity found in the vertebrate kingdom.

Left: A herd of springboks rest on an African grassland. These wild grasslands host the largest populations of grazing beasts on Earth. The springboks are known for "pronking" – leaping high into the air – when predators attack.

EVOLUTION

Animals and other forms of life did not just suddenly appear on the Earth. They evolved over billions of years into countless different forms. The mechanism by which they evolved is called natural selection. The process of natural selection was first proposed by British naturalist Charles Darwin.

Many biologists estimate that there are approximately 30 million species on Earth, but to date only about two million have been discovered and recorded by scientists. So where are the rest? They live in a staggering array of habitats, from the waters of the deep oceans where sperm whales live to the deserts of Mexico, inhabited by the powerful, poisonous, gila monster lizard. The problems faced by animals in these and other habitats on Earth are very different, and so life has evolved in great variety. Each animal needs a body that can cope with its own environment.

Past evidence

At the turn of the 19th century, geologists began to realize that the world was extremely old. They used animal fossils – usually the hard remains, such as shells and bones, which are preserved in stone – to measure the age of the exposed layers of rock found in cliffs and canyons. Today we accept that the Earth is about 4.5 billion years old, but in the early 1800s the idea that

the world was unimaginably old began to change people's ideas about the origins of life completely.

In addition, naturalists had always known that there was a fantastic variety of animals, but now they realized that many could be grouped into families, as if they were related. By the middle of 19th century, two British biologists had independently formulated an idea that would change the way that people saw themselves and the natural world forever. Charles Darwin and Alfred Wallace thought that the world's different animal species had gradually evolved from extinct relatives, like the ones preserved as fossils.

Darwin was the first to publish his ideas, in 1859. He had formulated them while touring South America where he studied the differences between varieties of finches and giant tortoises on the Galápagos Islands in the Pacific Ocean. Wallace came up with similar ideas about the same time, when studying different animals on the islands of South-east Asia and New Guinea.

Above: Scientists know about extinct animals from studying fossils such as these mammoth bones. Fossils are the remains of dead plants or animals that have been turned to stone by natural processes over millions of years.

Survival of the fittest

Both came up with the same idea – natural selection. As breeders had known for generations, animals pass on their characteristics to their young. Darwin and Wallace suggested that wild animal species also gradually evolved through natural selection, a similar system to the artificial selection that people were using to breed prize cattle, sheep and pedigree dogs.

The theory of natural selection is often described as the survival of the fittest. This is because animals must compete with each other for limited resources including food, water, shelter and mates. But they are not all equal or exactly similar, and some members of a population of animals will have characteristics which make them "fitter" – better suited to the environment at that time.

The fitter animals will therefore be more successful at finding food and avoiding predators. Consequently, they will probably produce more offspring, many of which will also have the same characteristics as their fit parents. Because of this, the next generation

---

Jumping animals

Most animals can leap into the air, but thanks to natural selection this simple ability has been harnessed by different animals in different ways. For example, click beetles jump in somersaults to frighten off attackers, while blood-sucking fleas can leap enormous heights to move from host to host.

Above: The flying frog uses flaps of skin between its toes to glide. This allows these tree-living frogs to leap huge distances between branches.

Above: This Thomson's gazelle is pronking, that is, leaping in high arcs to escape a chasing predator. Pronking makes it harder for predators to bring the antelope down.

will contain more individuals with the "fit" trait. And after many generations, it is possible that the whole population will carry the fit trait, since those without it die out.

Variation and time

The environment is not fixed, and does not stay the same for long. Volcanoes, diseases and gradual climate changes, for example, alter the conditions which animals have to confront. Natural selection relies on the way in which different individual animals cope with these changes. Those individuals that were once fit may later die out, as others that have a different set of characteristics become more successful in the changed environment.

Darwin did not know it, but parents pass their features on to their young through their genes. During sexual reproduction, the genes of both parents are jumbled up to produce a new individual with a unique set of characteristics. Every so often the genes mutate into a new form, and these mutations are the source of all new variations.

As the process of natural selection continues for millions of years, so groups of animals can change radically, giving rise to a new species. Life is thought to have been evolving for 3.5 billion years. In that time natural selection has produced a staggering number of species, with everything from oak trees to otters and coral to cobras.

A species is a group of organisms that can produce offspring with each other. A new species occurs once animals have changed so much that they are unable to breed with their ancestors. And if the latter no longer exist, then they have become extinct.

New species may gradually arise out of a single group of animals. In fact the original species may be replaced by one or more new species. This can happen when two separate groups of one species are kept apart by an impassable geographical feature, such as an ocean or mountain range. Kept isolated from each other, both groups then evolve in different ways and end up becoming new species.

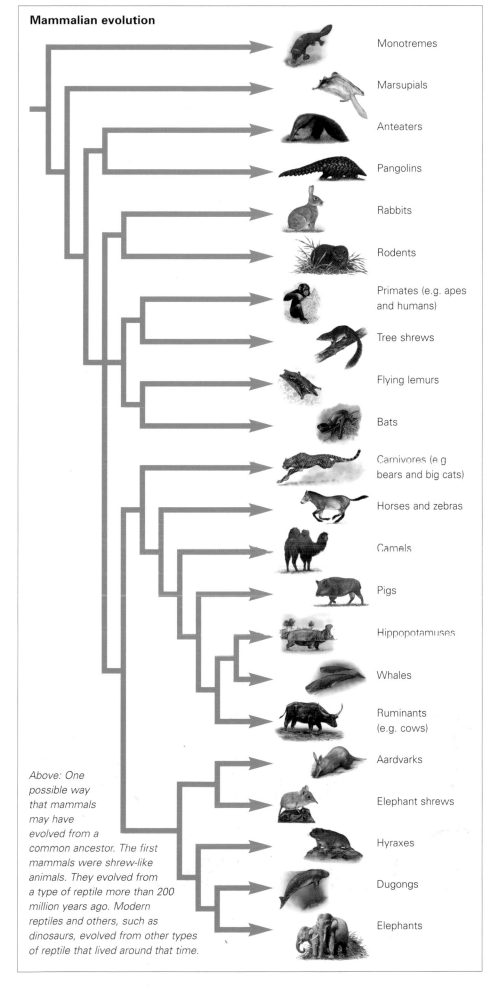

Mammalian evolution

Monotremes
Marsupials
Anteaters
Pangolins
Rabbits
Rodents
Primates (e.g. apes and humans)
Tree shrews
Flying lemurs
Bats
Carnivores (e.g. bears and big cats)
Horses and zebras
Camels
Pigs
Hippopotamuses
Whales
Ruminants (e.g. cows)
Aardvarks
Elephant shrews
Hyraxes
Dugongs
Elephants

Above: One possible way that mammals may have evolved from a common ancestor. The first mammals were shrew-like animals. They evolved from a type of reptile more than 200 million years ago. Modern reptiles and others, such as dinosaurs, evolved from other types of reptile that lived around that time.

ANATOMY

Mammals, reptiles and amphibians (which are vertebrates, as are fish and birds), come in a mind-boggling array of shapes and sizes. However all of them, from whales to bats and frogs to snakes, share a basic body plan, both inside and out.

Vertebrates are animals with a spine, generally made of bone. Bone, the hard tissues of which contain chalky substances, is also the main component of the rest of the vertebrate skeleton. The bones of the skeleton link together to form a rigid frame to protect organs and give the body its shape, while also allowing it to move. Cartilage, a softer, more flexible but tough tissue is found, for example, at the ends of bones in mobile joints, in the ears and the nose (forming the sides and the partition between the two nostrils). Some fish, including sharks and rays, have skeletons that consist entirely of cartilage.

Nerves and muscles

Vertebrates also have a spinal cord, a thick bundle of nerves extending from the brain through the spine, and down into the tail. The nerves in the spinal cord are used to control walking and other reflex movements. They also coordinate blocks of muscle that work together for an animal to move properly. A vertebrate's skeleton is on the inside, in contrast to many invertebrates, which have an outer skeleton or exoskeleton.

The vertebrate skeleton provides a solid structure which the body's muscles pull against. Muscles are blocks of protein that can contract and relax when they get an electrical impulse from a nerve.

Invertebrates

The majority of animals are invertebrates. They are a much more varied group than the vertebrates and include creatures as varied as shrimps, slugs, butterflies and starfish. Although some squid are thought to reach the size of a small whale, and while octopuses are at least as intelligent as cats and dogs, most invertebrates are much smaller and simpler animals than the vertebrates.

Below: The most successful invertebrates are the insects, including ants. This soldier army ant is defending workers as they collect food.

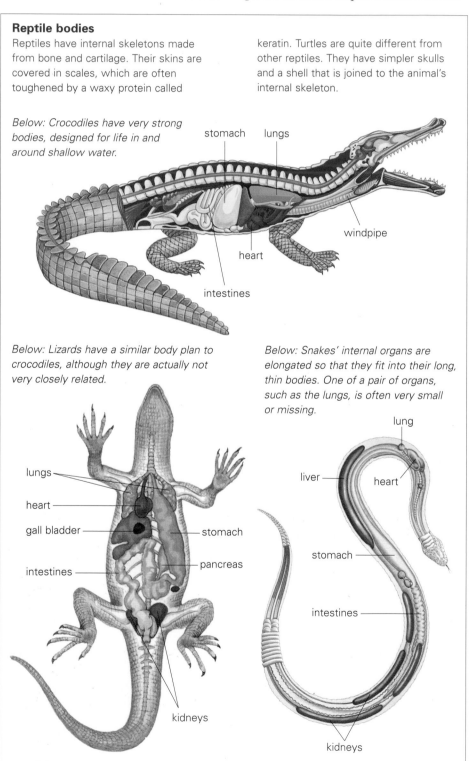

Reptile bodies

Reptiles have internal skeletons made from bone and cartilage. Their skins are covered in scales, which are often toughened by a waxy protein called keratin. Turtles are quite different from other reptiles. They have simpler skulls and a shell that is joined to the animal's internal skeleton.

Below: Crocodiles have very strong bodies, designed for life in and around shallow water.

stomach · lungs · windpipe · heart · intestines

Below: Lizards have a similar body plan to crocodiles, although they are actually not very closely related.

lungs · heart · gall bladder · intestines · stomach · pancreas · kidneys

Below: Snakes' internal organs are elongated so that they fit into their long, thin bodies. One of a pair of organs, such as the lungs, is often very small or missing.

lung · liver · heart · stomach · intestines · kidneys

When on the move, the vertebrate body works like a system of pulleys, pivots and levers. The muscles are the engines of the body, and are attached to bones – the levers – by strong cables called tendons. The joint between two bones forms a pivot, and the muscles work in pairs to move a bone. For example, when an arm is bent at the elbow to raise the forearm, the bicep muscle on the front of the upper arm has to contract. This pulls the forearm up, while the tricep muscle attached to the back of the upper arm remains relaxed. To straighten the arm again, the tricep contracts and the bicep relaxes. If both muscles contract at the same time, they pull against each other, and the arm remains locked in whatever position it is in.

Vital organs

Muscles are not only attached to the skeleton. The gut – including the stomach and intestines – is surrounded by muscles. These muscles contract in rhythmic waves to push food and waste products through the body. The heart is a muscular organ made of a very strong muscle which keeps on contracting and relaxing, pumping blood around the body. The heart and other vital organs are found in the thorax, that part of the body which lies between the forelimbs. In reptiles and mammals the thorax is kept well protected inside a rib cage, as are the lungs, liver and kidneys.

Vertebrates have a single liver consisting of a number of lobes. The liver has a varied role, making chemicals required by the body and storing food. Most vertebrates also have two kidneys. Their role is to clean the blood of any impurities and toxins, and to remove excess water. The main toxins that have to be removed are compounds containing nitrogen, the by-products of eating protein. Mammal and amphibian kidneys dissolve these toxins in water to make urine. However, since many reptiles live in very dry habitats, they cannot afford to use water to remove waste, and they instead get rid of it as a solid waste similar to bird excrement.

Mammalian bodies

Most mammals are four-limbed (exceptions being sea mammals such as whales). All have at least some hair on their bodies, and females produce milk. Mammals live in a wide range of habitats and their bodies are adapted in many ways to survive. Their internal organs vary depending on where they live and what they eat.

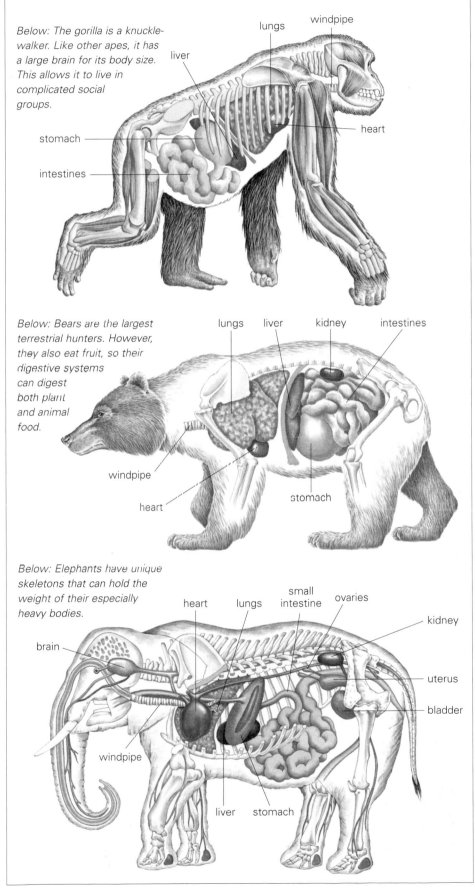

Below: The gorilla is a knuckle-walker. Like other apes, it has a large brain for its body size. This allows it to live in complicated social groups.

lungs
windpipe
liver
heart
stomach
intestines

Below: Bears are the largest terrestrial hunters. However, they also eat fruit, so their digestive systems can digest both plant and animal food.

lungs liver kidney intestines
windpipe
heart
stomach

Below: Elephants have unique skeletons that can hold the weight of their especially heavy bodies.

brain
heart lungs small intestine ovaries
kidney
uterus
bladder
windpipe
liver stomach

SENSES

To stay alive, animals must find food and shelter, and defend themselves against predators. To achieve these things, they are equipped with an array of senses for monitoring their surroundings. Different species have senses adapted to nocturnal or diurnal (day-active) life.

An animal's senses are its early-warning system. They alert it to changes in its surroundings – changes which may signal an opportunity to feed or mate, or the need to escape imminent danger. The ability to act quickly and appropriately is made possible because the senses are linked to the brain by a network of nerves which send messages as electric pulses. When the brain receives the information from the senses it coordinates its response.

In many cases, generally in response to something touching the body, the signal from the sensor does not reach the brain before action is taken. Instead, it produces a reflex response which is hardwired into the nervous system. For example, when you touch a very hot object, your hand automatically recoils; you don't need to think about it.

All animals have to be sensitive to their environment to survive. Even the simplest animals, such as jellyfish and roundworms, react to changes in their surroundings. Simple animals, however, have only a limited ability to move or defend themselves, and therefore generally have limited senses. Larger animals, such as vertebrates,

have a much more complex array of sense organs. Most vertebrates can hear, see, smell, taste and touch.

Vision

Invertebrates' eyes are generally designed to detect motion. Vertebrates' eyes, however, are better at forming clear images, often in colour. Vertebrates' eyes are balls of clear jelly which have an inner lining of light-sensitive cells. This lining, called the retina, is made up of one or two types of cell. The rod cells – named after their shape – are very sensitive to all types of light, but are only capable of forming black and white images. Animals which are active at night generally have (and need) only rods in their eyes.

Colour vision is important for just a few animals, such as monkeys, which need, for example, to see the brightest and therefore ripest fruits. Colour images are made by the cone cells – so named because of their shape – in the retina. There are three types of cone, each of which is sensitive to a particular wavelength of light. Low wavelengths appear as reds, high wavelengths as blues, with green colours being detected in between.

Above: Frogs have large eyes positioned on the upper side of the head so that the animals can lie mainly submerged in water with just their eyes poking out.

The light is focused on the retina by a lens to produce a clear image. Muscles change the shape of the lens so that it can focus the light arriving from different distances. While invertebrates may have several eyes, all vertebrates have just two, and they are always positioned on the head. Animals such as rabbits, which are constantly looking out for danger, have eyes on the side of the head to give a wide field of vision. But while they can see in almost all directions, rabbits have difficulty judging distances and speeds. Animals that have eyes pointing forward are better at doing this because each eye's field of vision overlaps with the other. This binocular vision helps hunting animals and others, such as tree-living primates, to judge distances more accurately.

Eyes can also detect radiation in a small band of wavelengths, and some animals detect radiation that is invisible to our eyes. Flying insects and birds can see ultraviolet light, which extends the range of their colour vision. At the other end of the spectrum many snakes can detect radiation with a lower wavelength. They sense infrared, or heat, through pits on the face which enables them to track their warm-blooded prey in pitch darkness.

Below: The lion's golden eyes are able to reflect light back through the retina, giving the animal excellent night vision because the retina has two chances to catch the light.

Below: Like other hunters, a seal has eyes positioned on the front of its head. Forward-looking eyes are useful for judging distances, making it easier to chase down prey.

Hearing

An animal's brain interprets waves of pressure travelling through the air, and detected by the ears, as sound. Many animals do not hear these waves with ears but detect them in other ways instead. For example, although snakes can hear, they are much more sensitive to vibrations through the lower jaw, travelling through the ground. Long facial whiskers sported by many mammals, from cats to dugongs, are very sensitive touch receptors. They can be so sensitive that they will even respond to currents in the air.

In many ways, hearing is a sensitive extension of the sense of touch. The ears of amphibians, reptiles and mammals have an eardrum which is sensitive to tiny changes in pressure. An eardrum is a thin membrane of skin which vibrates as the air waves hit it. A tiny bone (or in the case of mammals, three bones) attached to the drum transmit the vibrations to a shell-shaped structure called a cochlea. The cochlea is filled with a liquid which picks up the vibrations. As the liquid moves inside the cochlea, tiny hair-like structures lining it wave back and forth. Nerves stimulated by this wave motion send the information to the brain, which interprets it as sound.

A mammal's ear is divided into three sections. The cochlea forms the inner ear and the middle ear consists of the bones between the cochlea and eardrum. The outer ear is the tube joining the outside world and the

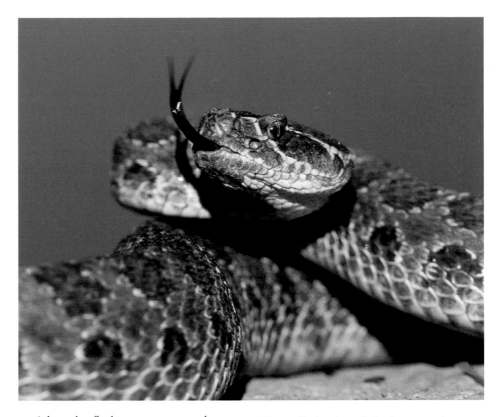

Above: Snakes have forked tongues that they use to taste the air. The tips of the fork are slotted into an organ in the roof of the mouth. This organ is linked to the nose, and chemicals picked up by the tongue are identified with great sensitivity.

auricle – the fleshy structure on the side of the head that collects the sound waves – to the middle ear. Amphibians and reptiles do not possess auricles. Instead their eardrums are either on the side of the head – easily visible on many frogs and lizards – or under the skin, as in snakes.

Smell and taste

Smell and taste are so closely related as to form a single sense. Snakes and lizards, for example, taste the air with their forked tongues. However, it is perhaps the most complex sense. Noses, tongues and other smelling

organs are lined with sensitive cells which can analyze a huge range of chemicals that float in the air or exist in food. Animals such as dogs, which rely on their sense of smell, have long noses packed with odour-sensitive cells. Monkeys, of the other hand, are less reliant on a sense of smell, and consequently have short noses capable only of detecting stronger odours.

Below: Hares have very large outer ears which they use like satellite dishes to pick up sound waves. They can rotate each ear separately to detect sound from all directions.

Below: Lizards do not have outer ears at all. Their hearing organs are contained inside the head and joined to the outside world through an eardrum membrane.

Below: Aardwolves have an excellent sense of smell and taste. They communicate with pack members and rival packs by smell, as part of a complex set of social behaviours.

SURVIVAL

In order to stay alive, animals must not only find enough food, but also avoid becoming a predator's meal. To achieve this, animals have evolved many strategies to feed on a wide range of foods, and an array of weapons and defensive tactics to keep safe.

An animal must keep feeding in order to replace the energy used in staying alive. Substances in the food, such as sugars, are burned by the body, and the subsequent release of energy is used to heat the body and power its movements. Food is also essential for growth. Although most growth takes place during the early period of an animal's life, it never really stops because injuries need to heal and worn-out tissues need replacing. Some animals continue growing throughout life. Proteins in the food are the main building blocks of living bodies.

Plant food

Some animals will eat just about anything, while others are much more fussy. As a group, vertebrates get their energy from a wide range of sources – everything from shellfish and wood to honey and blood. Animals are often classified according to how they feed, forming several large groups filled with many otherwise unrelated animals.

Animals that eat plants are generally grouped together as herbivores. But this term is not very descriptive because there is such a wide range of plant foods. Animals that eat grass are known as grazers. However, this term can also apply to any animal which eats any plant that covers the ground

Above: Impala are grazers. They eat grass and plants that grow close to the ground. Because their food is all around them, grazers spend a long time out in the open. They feed together in large herds since there is safety in numbers.

in large amounts, such as seaweed or sedge. Typical grazers include bison and wildebeest but some, such as the marine iguana or gelada baboon, are not so typical. Animals such as giraffes or antelopes, which pick off the tastiest leaves, buds and fruit from bushes and trees, are called browsers. Other browsing animals include many monkeys, but some monkeys eat only leaves (the folivores) or fruit (the frugivores).

Many monkeys have a much broader diet, eating everything from insects to the sap which seeps out from the bark of tropical trees. Animals that eat both plant and animal foods are called omnivores. Bears are omnivorous, as are humans, but the most catholic of tastes belong to scavenging animals, such as rats and other rodents, which eat anything they can get their teeth into. Omnivores in general, and scavengers in particular, are very curious animals. They will investigate anything that looks or smells like food, and if it also tastes like food, then it probably is.

A taste for flesh

The term carnivore is often applied to any animal that eats flesh, but it is more correctly used to refer to an order of mammals which includes cats, dogs, bears and many smaller animals, such as weasels and mongooses. These animals are the kings of killing, armed with razor-sharp claws and powerful jaws crammed full of chisel-like teeth. They use their strength and speed to overpower their prey, either by running them down or taking them by surprise with an ambush.

Below: Zebras are browsers, not grazers. They will eat some grass but also pick tastier leaves, buds and fruit off trees and shrubs. They often live in herds to stay safe from attack.

Below: Lions are unusual cats because they live together in prides. The members of the pride cooperate to catch food. They hunt as a team and share the food between them.

Above: African elephants have few predators. Younger elephants are at risk of leopard attacks, and the adults defend them by trumpeting, stamping and flapping their large ears. If that fails, they will charge.

However, land-dwelling carnivores are not the only expert killers. The largest meat-eater is the orca, or killer whale, which is at least three times the size of the brown bear, the largest killer on land.

While snakes are much smaller in comparison, they are just as deadly, if not more so. They kill in one of two ways, either suffocating their prey by wrapping their coils tightly around them, or by injecting them with a poison through their fangs.

Arms race

Ironically, the same weapons used by predators are often used by their prey to defend themselves. For example, several species of frog, toad and salamander secrete poisons on to their skin. In some cases, such as the poison-dart frog, this poison is enough to kill any predator that tries to eat it, thus making sure that the killer won't repeat its performance. More often, though, a predator finds that its meal tastes horrible and remembers not to eat another one again. To remind the predators to keep away, many poisonous amphibians are brightly

coloured, which ensures that they are easily recognized.

Many predators rely on stealth to catch their prey, and staying hidden is part of the plan. A camouflaged coat, such as a tiger's stripes, helps animals blend into their surroundings. Many species also use this technique to ensure that they do not get eaten. Most freeze when danger approaches, and then scurry to safety as quickly as possible. Chameleons have taken camouflage to an even more sophisticated level as they can change the colour of their scaly skins, which helps them to blend in with their surrounding environment.

Plant-eating animals that live in the open cannot hide from predators that are armed with sharp teeth and claws. And the plant-eaters cannot rely on similar weapons to defend themselves. They are outgunned

Right: Chameleons have skin cells that can be opened and closed to make their skin colour change.

Filter-feeders

Some animals filter their food from water. The giant baleen whales do this, sieving tiny shrimp-like animals called krill out of great gulps of sea water. Some tadpoles and larval salamanders filter-feed as well, extracting tiny plant-like animals which float in fresh water. However, after becoming adults, all amphibians become hunters and eat other animals. All snakes and most lizards are meat-eaters, or carnivores, as well.

Below: The largest animals of all, baleen whales, are filter-feeders. They do not have teeth. Instead, their gums are lined with a thick curtain of baleen that filters out tiny shrimp-like krill from sea water.

because they do not possess sharp, pointed teeth but flattened ones to grind up their plant food. The best chance they have of avoiding danger is to run away. Animals such as antelopes or deer consequently have long, hoofed feet that lengthen their legs considerably; they are, in fact, standing on their toenails. These long legs allow them to run faster and leap high into the air to escape an attacker's jaws.

Animals that do not flee must stand and fight. Most large herbivores are armed with horns or antlers. Although used chiefly for display, the horns are the last line of defence when cornered.

REPRODUCTION

All animals share the urge to produce offspring which will survive after the parents die. The process of heredity is determined by genes, through which characteristics are passed from parents to offspring. Reproduction presents several problems, and animals have adopted different strategies for tackling them.

Animals have two main goals: to find food and a mate. To achieve these goals, they must survive everything that the environment throws at them, from extremes of the weather, such as floods and droughts, to hungry predators. They have to find sufficient supplies of food, and on top of that locate a mate before their competitors. If they find sufficient food but fail to produce any offspring, their struggle for survival will have been wasted.

One parent or two?

There are two ways in which an animal can reproduce, asexually or sexually. Animals that are produced by asexual reproduction, or parthenogenesis, have only one parent, a mother. The offspring are identical to their mother and to each other. Sexual reproduction involves two parents of the opposite sex. The offspring are hybrids of the two parents, with a mixture of their parents' characteristics.

The offspring inherit their parents' traits through their genes. Genes can be defined in various ways. One simple definition is that they are the unit of inheritance – a single inherited

Above: Many male frogs croak by pumping air into an expandable throat sac. The croak is intended to attract females. The deeper the croak, the more attractive it is. However, some males lurk silently and mate with females as they approach the croaking males.

characteristic which cannot be subdivided any further. Genes are also segments of DNA (deoxyribonucleic acid), a complex chemical that forms long chains. It is found at the heart of every living cell. Each link in the DNA chain forms part of a code that controls how an animal's body develops and survives. And every cell in the body contains a full set of DNA which could be used to build a whole new body.

Animals produced through sexual reproduction receive half their DNA, or half their genes, from each parent. The male parent provides half the supply of genes, contained in a sperm. Each sperm's only role is to find its

Above: In deer and many other grazing animals, the males fight each other for the right to mate with the females in the herd. The deer with the largest antlers often wins without fighting, and real fights only break out if two males appear equally well-endowed.

way to, and fertilize, an egg, its female equivalent. Besides containing the other half of the DNA, the egg also holds a supply of food for the offspring as it develops into a new individual. Animals created through parthenogenesis get all their genes from their mother, and all of them are therefore the same sex – female.

Pros and cons

All mammals reproduce sexually, as do most reptiles and amphibians. However, there are a substantial number of reptiles and amphibians, especially lizards, which reproduce by parthenogenesis. There are benefits and disadvantages to both types of reproduction. Parthenogenesis is quick and convenient. The mother does not need to find a mate, and can devote all of her energy to producing huge numbers of young. This strategy is ideal for populating as yet unexploited territory. However, being identical, these animals are very vulnerable to attack. If, for example, one is killed by a disease or outwitted by a predator, it is very likely that they will all suffer the same fate. Consequently, whole communities of animals produced through parthenogenesis can be wiped out.

Below: Crocodiles bury their eggs in a nest. The temperature of the nest determines the sex of the young reptiles. Hot nests produce more males than cool ones. Crocodile mothers are very gentle when it comes to raising young.

Sexual animals, on the other hand, are much more varied. Each one is unique, formed by a mixture of genes from both parents. This variation means that a group of animals produced by sexual reproduction is more likely to triumph over adversity than a group of asexual ones. However, sexual reproduction takes up a great deal of time and effort.

Attracting mates

Since females produce only a limited number of eggs, they are keen to make sure that they are fertilized by a male with good genes. If a male is fit and healthy, this is a sign that he has good genes. Good genes will ensure that the offspring will be able to compete with other animals for food and mates of their own. Because the females have the final say in agreeing to mate, the

Above: Lions live in prides, in which one or two males father all the children. When a new adult takes control of the pride, he kills the cubs of his deposed rival so that the pride's females will be ready to mate with him sooner.

Below: Rhinoceroses are generally solitary animals, but offspring stay with their mother for at least a year while they grow big enough to look after themselves.

Above: Baboons are highly intelligent animals. Parents rear their offspring intensively while the young learn to survive the complexities and dangers of the savannah and rocky hills. The offspring stay with their mother for up to 18 months, often clinging to her back.

males have to put a lot of effort into getting noticed. Many are brightly coloured, make loud noises, and they are often larger than the females. In many species the males even compete with each other for the right to display to the females. Winning that right is a good sign that they have the best genes.

Parental care

The amount of care that the offspring receive from their parents varies considerably. There is a necessary trade-off between the amount of useful care parents can give to each offspring, the number of offspring they can produce and how regularly they can breed. Mammals invest heavily in parental care, suckling their young after giving birth, while most young amphibians or reptiles never meet their parents at all.

By suckling, mammals ensure that their young grow to a size where they can look after themselves. Generally, the young stay with the mother until it is time for her to give birth to the next litter – at least one or two months. However, in many species, including humans, the young stay with their parents for many years.

Other types of animals pursue the opposite strategy, producing large numbers of young that are left to fend for themselves. The vast majority in each batch of eggs – consisting of hundreds or even thousands – die before reaching adulthood, and many never even hatch. The survival rates, for example of frogs, are very low.

Animals that live in complicated societies, such as elephants, apes and humans, tend to produce a single offspring every few years. The parents direct their energies into protecting and rearing the young, giving them a good chance of survival. Animals which live for a only a short time, such as mice, rabbits, and reptiles and amphibians in general, need to reproduce quickly to make the most of their short lives. They produce high numbers of young, and do not waste time on anything more than the bare minimum of parental care. If successful, these animals can reproduce at an alarming pace.

AMPHIBIANS

Amphibians are the link between fish and land animals. One in eight of all vertebrate animals are amphibians. This group includes frogs, toads and newts as well as rarer types, such as giant sirens, hellbenders and worm-like caecilians. Amphibians are equally at home in water and on land.

Amphibians live on every continent except for Antarctica. None can survive in salt water, although a few species live close to the sea in the brackish water at river mouths. Being cold-blooded – their body temperature is always about the same as the temperature of their surroundings – most amphibians are found in the warmer regions of the world.

Unlike other land vertebrates, amphibians spend the early part of their lives in a different form from that of the adults. As they grow, the young gradually metamorphose into the adult body. Having a larval form means that the adults and their offspring live and feed in different places. In general the larvae are aquatic, while the adults spend most of their time on land.

The adults are hunters, feeding on other animals, while the young are generally plant eaters, filtering tiny plants from the water or grazing on aquatic plants which line the bottom of ponds and rivers.

Below: Amphibians must lay their eggs near a source of water. In most cases, such as this frog spawn, the eggs are laid straight into a pond or swamp. The tadpoles develop inside the jelly-like egg and then hatch out after the food supply in the egg's yolk runs out.

Life changing

Most amphibians hatch from eggs laid in water or, in a few cases, in moist soil or nests made of hardened mucus. Once hatched, the young amphibians, or larvae, live as completely aquatic animals. Those born on land wriggle to the nearest pool of water or drop from their nest into a river.

The larvae of frogs and toads are called tadpoles. Like the young of salamanders – a group that includes all other amphibians except caecilians – tadpoles do not have any legs at first. They swim using a long tail that has a fish-like fin extending along its length. As they grow, the larvae sprout legs. In general the back legs begin to grow first, followed by the front pair. Adult frogs do not have tails, and after the first few months a tadpole's tail begins to be reabsorbed into the body – it does not just fall away.

All adult salamanders keep their tails, and those species that spend their entire lives in water often retain the fin along the tail, along with other parts, such as external gills, a feature that is more commonly seen in the larval stage.

Above: Amphibians begin life looking very different from the adult form. Most of the time these larval forms, such as this frog tadpole, live in water as they slowly develop into the adult form, growing legs and lungs so that they can survive on land.

Body form

Amphibian larvae hatch with external gills but, as they grow, many (including all frogs and the many salamanders which live on land) develop internal gills. In most land-living species these internal gills are eventually replaced by lungs. Amphibians are also able to absorb oxygen directly through the skin, especially through the thin and moist tissues inside the mouth. A large number of land-living salamanders get all their oxygen in this way because they do not have lungs.

All adult frogs and toads return to the water to breed and lay their eggs, which are often deposited in a jelly-like mass called frog spawn. Several types of salamander do not lay eggs, and instead the females keep the fertilized eggs inside their bodies. The larvae develop inside the eggs, fed by a supply of rich yoke, and do not hatch until they have reached adult form.

Above: After the first few weeks, a tadpole acquires tiny back legs. As the legs grow, the long tail is gradually reabsorbed into the body. The front legs appear after the back ones have formed.

Adult form

Most adult amphibians have four limbs, with four digits on the front pair and five on the rear. Unlike other land-living animals, such as reptiles or mammals, their skin is naked and soft. Frogs' skin is smooth and moist, while toads generally have a warty appearance.

The skins of many salamanders are brightly coloured, with patterns that often change throughout the year. Colour change prior to the mating season signals the salamander's readiness to mate. Many frogs also have bright skin colours. Although their skin shades can change considerably in different light levels, these colours are generally not mating signals to fellow frogs. Instead they are warnings to predators that the frog's skin is laced with deadly poison. While toads tend to be drab in colour, many also secrete toxic chemicals to keep predators away. These substances are often stored in swollen warts which burst when the toad is attacked.

Below: Adult frogs may live in water or on land. Aquatic ones have webbed feet, while those on land have powerful legs for jumping and climbing. All frogs must return to a source of water to mate.

Forever young

Salamanders which have changed into adults, but which have not yet reached adult size, are called efts. The time it takes for an amphibian to grow from a newly hatched larva to an adult varies considerably, and the chief factor is the temperature of the water in which it is developing. Most frogs and toads develop in shallow waters, warmed by the summer sun, and they generally reach adulthood within three to four months. However, salamanders, especially the largest ones, can take much longer, and at the northern and southern limits of their geographical spread some salamanders stay as larvae for many years. It appears that the trigger for the change into adult form is linked to the temperature, and in cold climates this change happens only every few years. In fact it may not happen during a salamander's lifetime, and consequently several species have evolved the ability to develop sexual organs even when they still look like larvae.

Below: Marbled salamanders are unusual in that the females lay their eggs on dry land and coil themselves around them to keep them as moist as possible. They stay like this until the seasonal rains fall. The water stimulates the eggs to hatch.

REPTILES

Reptiles include lizards, snakes, alligators, crocodiles, turtles and tortoises, as well as now-extinct creatures such as dinosaurs and the ancestors of birds. Crocodiles have roamed the Earth for 200 million years and are still highly successful hunters.

Reptiles are a large and diverse group of animals containing about 6,500 species. Many of these animals look very different from each other and live in a large number of habitats, from the deep ocean to the scorching desert. Despite their great diversity, all reptiles share certain characteristics.

Most reptiles lay eggs, but these are different from those of an amphibian because they have a hard, thin shell rather than a soft, jelly-like one. This protects the developing young inside and, more importantly, stops them from drying out. Shelled eggs were an evolutionary breakthrough because they meant that adult reptiles did not have to return to the water to breed. Their waterproof eggs could be laid anywhere, even in the driest places. Reptiles were also the first group of land-living animals to develop into an adult form inside the egg. They did not emerge as under-developed larvae like the young of most amphibians.

Below: Alligators and other crocodilians are an ancient group of reptiles that have no close living relatives. They are archosaurs, a group of reptiles that included the dinosaurs. Other living reptiles belong to a different group.

Released from their ties to water, the reptiles developed unique ways of retaining moisture. Their skins are covered by hardened plates or scales to stop water being lost. The scales are also coated with the protein keratin, the same substance used to make fingernails and hair.

All reptiles breathe using lungs; if they were to absorb air through the skin it would involve too much water loss. Like amphibians, reptiles are cold-blooded and cannot heat their bodies from within as mammals can. Consequently, reptiles are commonly found in warm climates.

Ancient killers

Being such a diverse group, reptiles share few defining characteristics besides their shelled eggs, scaly skin and lungs. They broadly divide into four orders. The first contains the crocodiles, and includes alligators and caimans; these are contemporaries of the dinosaurs, both groups being related to a common ancestor.

In fact today's crocodiles have changed little since the age when dinosaurs ruled the world over 200 million years

Above: Turtles and their relatives, such as these giant tortoises, are unusual reptiles. Not only do they have bony shells fused around their bodies, but they also have skulls that are quite different from other reptiles. Turtles are also unusual because many of them live in the ocean, while most reptiles live on land.

ago. Unlike the dinosaurs, which disappeared 65 million years ago, the crocodiles are still going strong. Technically speaking, the dinosaurs never actually died out; their direct descendents, the birds, are still thriving. Although birds are now grouped separately from reptiles, scientists know that they all evolved from ancestors which lived about 400 million years ago. Mammals, on the other hand, broke away from this group about 300 million years ago.

Above: Most reptiles, including this tree boa, lay eggs. The young hatch looking like small versions of the adults. However, several snakes and lizards give birth to live young, which emerge from their mother fully formed.

Distant relatives

The second reptile order includes turtles, terrapins and tortoises. These are only distantly related to other reptiles, and it shows. Turtles are also the oldest group of reptiles, evolving their bony shells and clumsy bodies before crocodiles, dinosaurs or any other living reptile group existed. Although turtles evolved on land, many have since returned to water. However, they still breathe air, and all must return to land to lay their eggs.

The third group of reptiles is the largest. Collectively called the squamates, this group includes snakes and lizards.

Snakes, with their legless bodies and formidable reputations, are perhaps the most familiar reptiles. They evolved from animals that did have legs, and many retain tiny vestiges of legs. The squamates include other legless members such as the amphisbaenians (or worm lizards) and slow worms. Both of these groups are more closely related to lizards than snakes, despite looking more like the latter. Lizards are not a simple group of reptiles, and many biologists refer to them as several different groups, including the skinks, monitors, geckos and iguanas.

Below: Lizards, such as this iguana, are the largest group of reptiles. Most are hunters that live in hot parts of the world, and they are especially successful in dry areas where other types of animal are not so common.

The squamates are so diverse in their lifestyles and body forms that it is hard to find factors which they have in common. One feature not found in other reptile orders is the Jacobson's organ. It is positioned in the roof of the mouth and is closely associated with the nose. All snakes and most lizards use this organ to "taste" the air and detect prey. The long forked tongue of most of these animals flicks out into the air, picking up tiny particles on its moist surface. Once back inside the mouth, each fork slots into the Jacobson's organ which then analyzes the substances.

The fourth and final order of reptiles is very small: the tuataras. These include just a few species, all of which are very rare indeed, clinging to life on islands off the mainland of New Zealand. To most people a tuatara looks like a large iguana. However, scientists believe that it is only a distant relative of lizards and other squamates because it has an odd-shaped skull and no eardrums.

Tuatara

Despite their differences from lizards and other squamates, tuataras do share one feature with lizards: the so-called third eye. This light-sensitive gland inside the head can detect light penetrating the thin skull. Both types of reptile use the third eye to regulate their exposure to the sun and so regulate their body temperature throughout the year.

Below: The tuatara is a living fossil, living on just a few islands around New Zealand. It looks like a lizard, but its skull and skeleton show that it is the last member of another ancient group of reptiles.

PLACENTAL MAMMALS

Mammals are the most familiar of all vertebrates. This is because not only are human beings mammals, but also most domestic animals and pets belong in this category. Placental mammals are also more widespread than other types of animal, being found in all parts of the world.

Mammals are grouped together because they share a number of characteristics. However, these common features do not come close to describing the huge diversity within the mammal class. For example, the largest animal that has ever existed on Earth – the blue whale – is a mammal, and so this monster of the deep shares several crucial traits with even the smallest mammals, such as the tiniest of shrews. Other mammals include elephants and moles, monkeys and hippopotamuses, and bats and camels. To add to this great diversity, mammals live in more places on Earth than any other group of animals, from the frozen ice fields of the Arctic to the humid treetops of the Amazon rainforest, and even under the sandy soil of African deserts.

Mammal bodies

The most obvious mammalian feature is hair. All mammals have hair made of keratin protein and, in most cases, it forms a thick coat of fur, though many

Below: Although they are often mistaken for fish, dolphins are mammals: they breathe air and suckle their young. However, life under water requires flippers and fins, not legs.

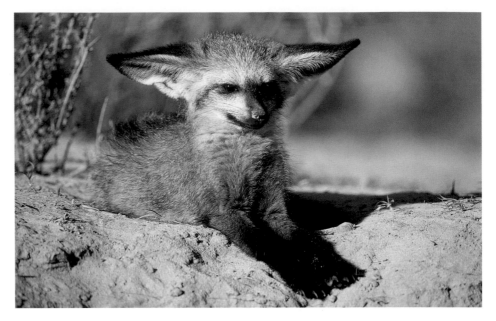

Above: The bat-eared fox has adapted to life in warm open country by having huge ears which not only radiate excess heat but also provide the animal with very sensitive hearing, useful for detecting the movements of very small prey such as harvester termites.

mammals are relatively naked, not least humans. Unlike reptiles and amphibians, all mammals are warm-blooded, which means that they can keep their body temperature at a constant level. While this requires quite a lot of energy, it means that mammals are not totally dependent on the temperature of their surroundings. In places where other vertebrates would be frozen solid, mammals can survive by seeking out food and keeping themselves warm. Many mammals, including humans, can also cool their bodies using sweat. The water secreted on the skin cools the body efficiently, but it does mean that these animals need to drink more replacement water than do other groups.

Incidentally, the name mammal comes from the mammary glands. These glands are the means by which all female mammals provide milk (or liquid food) to their developing young. The young suck the milk through teats or nipples for the first few weeks or months of life.

Reproduction

Mammals reproduce in a number of ways. Monotremes, such as the duck-billed platypus, lay eggs, but all other mammals give birth to their young. Marsupials, a relatively small group of animals which includes kangaroos, give birth to very undeveloped young which then continue to grow inside a fold or pouch on the mother's skin.

The majority of mammals, called the placental mammals or eutherians, do not give birth to their young until they are fully formed and resemble the adults. The developing young, or foetuses, grow inside a womb or uterus where they are fed by the mother through a placenta. This large organ allows the young to stay inside the mother for a lot longer than in most other animals. It forms the interface between the mother's blood supply and that of the developing foetus, where oxygen and food pass from the parent to her offspring. The placenta is attached to the foetus by means of an umbilical cord which withers and drops off soon after the birth.

Widespread range

Mammals are found in a wider variety of habitats than any other group of animals. While mammals all breathe air with their

Right: One factor that makes mammals unique is that the females have mammary glands. These glands produce milk for the young animals to drink, as this fallow deer fawn is doing. The milk is a mixture of fat, protein and sugars.

Above: Elephants are the largest land mammals in the world. They are most closely related to rabbit-like hyraxes and walrus-like dugongs and manatees.

lungs, this has not prevented many from making their homes in water. In many ways the streamlined bodies of whales and dolphins, for example, resemble those of sharks and other large fish. However, they are very much mammals, breathing air through a large nostril or blowhole in the top of the head, but their body hair has been reduced to just a few thick bristles.

Above: Plenty of mammals can glide, but only bats join birds and insects in true flight. A bat wing is made from skin that is stretched between long finger bones.

At the other end of the spectrum, some mammals even fly. Bats darting through the gloom of a summer evening may appear to be small birds, but they too are mammals with furry bodies and wings made from stretched skin instead of feathers. Although most other mammals have a more conventional body plan, with four legs and a tail, they too have evolved to survive in a startling range of habitats. They have achieved this not just by adapting their bodies but by changing their behaviour. In general, mammals have larger brains than reptiles and amphibians, and this allows them to understand their environment more fully. Many mammals, such as monkeys and dogs, survive by living in complex social groups in which individuals cooperate with each other when hunting food, protecting the group from danger and even finding mates.

ECOLOGY

Ecology is the study of how groups of organisms interact with members of their own species, other organisms and the environment. All types of animals live in a community of interdependent organisms called an ecosystem, in which they have their own particular role.

The natural world is filled with a wealth of opportunities for animals to feed and breed. Every animal species has evolved to take advantage of a certain set of these opportunities, called a niche. A niche is not just a physical place but also a lifestyle exploited by that single species. For example, even though they live in the same rainforest habitat, sloths and tapirs occupy very different niches.

To understand how different organisms interrelate, ecologists combine all the niches in an area into a community, called an ecosystem. Ecosystems do not really exist because it is impossible to know where one ends and another begins, but the system is a useful tool when learning more about the natural world.

Food chains

One way of understanding how an ecosystem works is to follow the food chains within it. A food chain is made up of a series of organisms that prey on each other. Each habitat is filled with them, and since they often merge into and converge from each other, they are often combined into food webs.

Below: The lion is at the top of a very simple food chain: lions eat zebras, and zebras eat grass. For this reason, there are fewer lions than there are zebras, and there are fewer zebras than there is grass.

Ecologists use food chains to see how energy and nutrients flow through natural communities. Food chains always begin with plants. Plants are the only organisms on Earth that do not need to feed, deriving their energy from sunlight, whereas all other organisms, including animals, get theirs from food. At the next level up the food chain come the plant-eaters. They eat the plants, and extract the sugar and other useful substances made by them. And, like the plants, they use these substances to power their bodies and stay alive. The predators occupy the next level up, and they eat the bodies of the plant-eating animals.

At each stage of the food chain, energy is lost, mainly as heat given out by the animals' bodies. Because of this, less energy is available at each level up the food chain. This means that in a healthy ecosystem there are always fewer predators than prey, and always more plants than plant-eaters.

Nutrient cycles

A very simple food chain would be as follows: grass, wildebeest and lion. However, the reality of most ecosystems is much more complex, with many more layers, including certain animals that eat both plants and animals. Every food chain ends with a top predator, in our example, the lion. Nothing preys on the lion, at least when it is alive, but once it dies the food chain continues as insects, fungi and other decomposers feed on the carcass. Eventually nothing is left of the lion's body. All the energy stored in it is removed by the decomposers, and the chemicals which made up its body have returned to the environment as carbon dioxide gas, water and minerals in the soil. And these are the very same substances needed by a growing plant. The cycle is complete.

Above: Nothing is wasted in nature. The dung beetle uses the droppings of larger grazing animals as a supply of food for its developing young. Since the beetles clear away all the dung, the soil is not damaged by it, the grass continues to grow, and the grazers have plenty of food.

Living together

As food chains show, the lives of different animals in an ecosystem are closely related. If all the plants died for some reason, it would not just be the plant-eaters that would go hungry. As all of them begin to die, the predators would starve too. Only the decomposers might appear to benefit. Put another way, the other species living alongside an animal are just as integral to that animal's environment as the weather and landscape. This is yet another way of saying that animal species have not evolved isolated from each another.

The result is that as predators have evolved new ways of catching their prey, the prey has had to evolve new ways of escaping. On many occasions this process of co-evolution has created symbiotic relationships between two different species. For example, honeyguide birds lead badgers to bees' nests.

Some niches are very simple, and the animals that occupy them live simple, solitary lives. Others, especially those occupied by mammals, are much more complex and require members of a species to live closely together. These aggregations of animals may be simple herds or more structured social groups.

Food chain

Food chains show how the energy needed for life passes through an ecosystem. The energy originates in the Sun. This makes plants grow, which are then eaten by animals. The plant-eating animals then become meals themselves.

Below: This food chain shows what animals eat in a temperate country, such as Britain. Herbivores eat only plants, while carnivores eat mainly other animals. Animals that eat both plants and animals are omnivores – for example, humans.

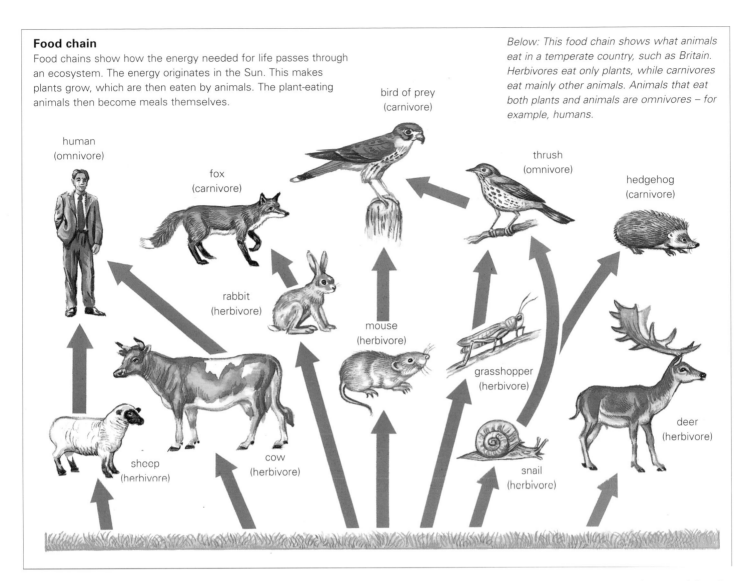

human (omnivore)

bird of prey (carnivore)

fox (carnivore)

thrush (omnivore)

hedgehog (carnivore)

rabbit (herbivore)

mouse (herbivore)

grasshopper (herbivore)

deer (herbivore)

sheep (herbivore)

cow (herbivore)

snail (herbivore)

Group living

A herd, flock or shoal is a group of animals which gathers together for safety. Each member operates as an individual, but is physically safest in the centre of the group, the danger of attack being greatest on the edge. Herd members do not actively communicate dangers to each other. When one is startled by something and bolts, the rest will probably follow.

Members of a social group, on the other hand, work together to find food, raise their young and defend themselves. Many mammals, for example apes, monkeys, dogs, dolphins and elephants, form social groups, and these groups exist in many forms. At one end of the spectrum are highly ordered societies, such as lion prides and baboon troops, which are often controlled by one dominant male, the other members often having their own ranking in a strict hierarchical structure. At the other end of the spectrum are leaderless gangs of animals, such as squirrel monkeys, which merge and split with no real guiding purpose.

There are many advantages of living in social groups, with members finding more food and being warned of danger, for example. However, in many societies only a handful of high-ranking members are allowed to breed. In these cases, the groups are held together by a complex fusion of family ties in which brothers and sisters help to raise nephews and nieces. Politics also plays its cohesive part, with members forming and breaking alliances in order to rise to the top.

Below: Meerkats live in family groups called bands. They need to live together because they live in a dry habitat where they must cooperate to find food, raise young and avoid being eaten by predators.

MIGRATION AND HIBERNATION

Migration and hibernation are two ways in which animals cope with the changing seasons and fluctuations in the supply of food. By hibernating, they sleep through periods of bad weather when food is hard to find, and by migrating, they reach places where food is more readily available.

Everywhere on Earth, the climate changes throughout the year with the cycle of seasons. In some places these changes are hardly noticeable from month to month, while in others each new season brings extremes of weather from blistering hot summers to freezing winters, or torrential rains followed by drought.

Change of lifestyle

In temperate regions, such as Europe, the year is generally divided into four seasons. Other regions experience a different annual cycle of changes. For example, tropical regions do not really have fluctuating temperatures, but many areas do experience periods of relative dry and at least one period of heavier rains each year. By contrast, in the far north, the change between the short summer and long winter is so quick that, in effect, there are only two seasons.

Above: Reptiles that live in cooler parts of the world – rattlesnakes, for example – spend a long time lying dormant. They do not hibernate like mammals, but because they are cold-blooded and do not need lots of energy to function, they can go for long periods without food.

Animals must, of course, react to these changes if they are to survive the harshest weather and make the most of clement conditions. Monkeys, for example, build up a mental map of their patch of forest so that they know where the fresh leaves will be after the rains, and where to find the hardier forest fruits during a drought. Wolves living in chilly northern forests hunt together in packs during the cold winter, working together to kill animals which are much larger than they are. However, when the summer arrives they tend to forage alone, picking off the many smaller animals, such as rodents and rabbits, which appear when the snow melts.

Hibernation

The reason the wolves find these smaller animals in the summer is that they suddenly emerge having passed the winter in cosy burrows or nests. This behaviour is commonly called hibernating, but there is a distinction between true hibernation and simply being inactive over winter.

Animals such as bears and tree squirrels are not true hibernators. Although they generally sleep for long periods during the coldest parts of winter, hunkered down in a den or

---

drey, they do not enter the deep, unconscious state of hibernation. Unable to feed while asleep, these animals rely on their bodily reserves of fat to stay alive. However, they often wake up during breaks in the harshest weather and venture outside to urinate or snatch a meal. Because tree squirrels have less fat reserves than bears, they frequently visit caches (stores) of food which they filled in the autumn.

On the other hand, the true hibernators, such as dormice or woodchucks, do not stir at all over winter. They rely completely on their reserves of fat to stay alive, and to save energy their metabolism slows to a fraction of its normal pace.

Only warm-blooded animals hibernate because they are the main types of animals which can survive in places where hibernation is necessary. However, rattlesnakes often pass the winter in rocky crevices and burrows. Reptiles and amphibians which live in very hot and dry places have their own form of hibernation, called aestivation.

Hibernating heart rate

The hibernating animal's heart rate slows to just a few beats per minute. It breathes more slowly and its body temperature drops to just a few degrees above the surrounding air temperature.

Below: The bodies of true hibernators, such as the dormouse, shut down almost completely during hibernation. Other hibernators, such as bears, may be out of sight for most of the winter, but they do not become completely dormant and their temperature does not fall drastically.

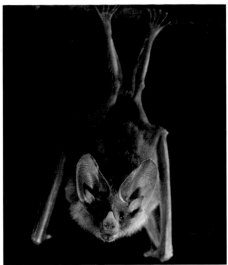

They become dormant when their habitat becomes too dry. Most bury themselves in moist sand or under rocks, only becoming active again when rain brings the habitat back to life. Some aestivating frogs even grow a skin cocoon which traps moisture and keeps their bodies moist while they wait for the rains to return.

Migration

Another way of coping with bad conditions is to migrate. Migrations are not just random wanderings, but involve following a set route each year. In general they are two-way trips, with animals returning to where they started once conditions back home become favourable again.

All sorts of animals migrate, from insects to whales, and there are many reasons for doing so. Most migrators are looking for supplies of food, or for a safe place to rear their young. For example, once their home territory becomes too crowded, young lemmings stampede over wide areas looking for new places to live, sometimes dying in the process. Herds of reindeer leave the barren tundra as winter approaches, and head for the relative warmth of the forest. Mountain goats act in a similar way: having spent the summer grazing in high alpine meadows, they descend below the treeline when winter snow begins to cover their pastures.

Other migrations are on a much grander scale, and in some cases an animal's whole life can be a continual migration. Wildebeest travel in huge

Above: Whales have the longest migrations of all mammals. They move from their warm breeding grounds near the Equator to feeding areas in cooler waters near the poles.

herds across southern Africa in search of fresh pastures. They follow age-old routes but may take a detour if grass is growing in unusual places. Among the greatest migrants are the giant whales, which travel thousands of miles from their breeding grounds in the tropics to their feeding grounds near the poles. The cool waters around the poles teem with plankton food, while the warmer tropical waters are a better place for giving birth.

Day length

How do animals know that it is time to hibernate or migrate? The answer lies in the changing number of hours of daylight as the seasons change.

All animals are sensitive to daylight, and use it to set their body clocks or circadian rhythms. These rhythms

Above: Bats spend long periods hibernating. They mate before winter, and the females store the sperm inside their body, only releasing it on the eggs as spring approaches.

affect all bodily processes, including the build-up to the breeding season. The hibernators begin to put on weight or store food as the days shorten, and many migrants start to get restless before setting off on their journey. However, not all migrations are controlled by the number of hours of daylight. Some migrators, such as wildebeest and lemmings, move because of other environmental factors, such as the lack of food caused by drought or overcrowding.

Below: The migrations of enormous herds of wildebeest across the huge grasslands of Africa is one of the natural wonders of the world. These large antelopes travel in search of watering holes and new areas of fresh grass. The migrations do not follow the same route each year, but the herds generally do stay on tried and tested trails.

ENDANGERED SPECIES

Many animals are threatened with extinction because they cannot survive in a world which is constantly being changed by human intervention. Many species have already become extinct, and if people do nothing to save them, a great many more will follow.

Surprising though it may sound, there is nothing unusual in extinctions, for they are an important part of the natural world. As the climate and landscape have changed in a given area over millions of years, the animals that live there have also changed. And as a new species evolves, so another is forced out of its habitat and becomes extinct. All that remains, if we are lucky, are a few fosslized bones – a record in stone.

Mass extinction?

Biologists estimate that there are at least several million species alive today, and possibly as many as 30 million. Whatever the figure, there are probably more species on Earth right now than at any other time. Therefore, because of the habitat destruction caused by people, more species are becoming extinct or are being threatened with extinction than ever before.

Geologists and biologists know that every now and then there are mass extinctions, in which great

Below: Okapis are rare mammals whose closest living relatives are giraffes, despite the zebra-stripes on their hindquarters and forelegs. They live in the forest of the Congo in central Africa. This forest has been ravaged by war and deforestation, and okapis and other forest-dwellers are now very rare.

Above: Leatherback turtles are the largest turtles in the world – even larger than the better-known giant tortoises. They are becoming rare because of the decline in untouched beaches on which to lay their eggs. Fewer leatherbacks are being born, and even fewer reach adulthood.

numbers of the world's animals die out forever. For example, it is widely believed that the dinosaurs and many other reptiles were wiped out after a meteorite smashed into Mexico 65 million years ago. But the questions are now: are we witnessing the natural world's latest mass extinction? And are humans the cause?

Most of the world's animal species are insects – especially beetles – and other invertebrates. It is likely that many of these species, especially those living in tropical forests, are becoming extinct. However, since scientists may never have had a chance to describe many of them, nobody knows the true number.

Life list

With vertebrate animals, it is a different story. Because there are only a few thousand species of animals with backbones, most of which have been recognized for hundreds of years, we know a great deal more about the plight of each species. Many species, for example mice, dogs and horses, thrive in a world dominated by people. However, a great many more species have suffered as people have destroyed their habitats, either deliberately or by upsetting the balance of nature by introducing species from other parts of the world.

The International Union for the Conservation of Nature and Natural Resources (IUCN) produces a Red List of animals which are in danger of extinction. There are currently about 5,500 animals listed in a number of categories, including extinct in the wild, endangered and vulnerable. Nearly one quarter of all mammals are included on the list, and about four per cent of reptiles and three of amphibians. However, while the status of all mammals has been assessed by the IUCN, only a fraction of reptiles and amphibians has been as thoroughly checked, and it is very likely that many more species are much closer to extinction than was previously thought.

Below: Over the past century, cheetah populations have declined rapidly. One of the main reasons for this is that humans have hunted them for their pelts, reducing their genetic diversity and making them more vulnerable to disease. In addition, much of their grassland habitat has been used for farming.

Above: Gorillas are endangered because their forest habitats are being destroyed. They are not able to thrive anywhere else. Also, these great apes are hunted for meat. Although illegal, the bush-meat trade is highly profitable, but soon there may be no gorillas left.

Wiped out

As the forests of Europe and China were cleared over the past thousand years, forest animals had increasingly fewer places to live. And as they inevitably came into increasingly close contact with people, wild animals, such as boars, bears and wolves, became persecuted and were eventually wiped out in many areas.

Above: All five species of rhinoceros are dangerously close to extinction in the wild. During the 1970s half of the world's population disappeared, and today less than 15 per cent of the 1970s population remains, an estimated 10,000 to 11,000 individuals.

As the world's human population soared in the 20th century, a similar process took place elsewhere. Another major habitat being destroyed was, and still is, the tropical rainforest. The number of species living in these areas is much higher than elsewhere, and a proportionately huge number of species are finding it harder to survive.

Although few animals on the Red List have actually become extinct, the situation is becoming graver for most species. The monkeys and apes of the tropical rainforests are among the worst affected, with nearly one in four species being very close to extinction. This is because rainforests are complicated places, and many primate species there have evolved a specialized lifestyle, for example feeding on fruit in the tallest trees. These species are very badly affected by sudden changes in their environment, for example when a logging team cuts down all the tall trees leaving, just the shorter ones behind.

CONSERVING WILDLIFE

With so many species facing extinction, conservationists have their work cut out. Conservationists try to protect habitats and provide safe places for threatened animals to thrive, but the activities of ordinary people can often also have an adverse effect on the future of natural habitats.

People give many reasons why wildlife should be conserved. Some argue that if all the forests were cleared and the oceans polluted, the delicate balance of nature would be so ruined that Earth would not be able to support any life, including humans. Others suggest that if vulnerable species were allowed to die, the natural world would not be sufficiently diverse to cope with future changes in the environment. Another reason to save diversity is that we have not yet fully recorded it. Also, there are undoubtedly many as yet unknown species – especially of plants – which could be useful to humankind, for example in the field of medicine. But perhaps the strongest argument for the conservation of wildlife is that it would be totally irresponsible to let it disappear.

Habitat protection

Whatever the reasons, the best way to protect species in danger of being wiped out is to protect their habitats so that the complex communities of

plants and animals can continue to live. However, with the human population growing so rapidly, people are often forced to choose between promoting their own interests and protecting wildlife. Of course, people invariably put themselves first, which means that the conservationists have to employ a range of techniques in order to save wildlife.

In many countries it has now become illegal to hunt certain endangered animals, or to trade in any products made from their bodies. Whales, gorillas and elephants are protected in this way. Many governments and charitable organizations have also set up wildlife reserves, where the animals stand a good chance of thriving. The oldest

Below: One of the main causes of deforestation is people clearing the trees and burning them to make way for farmland. The ash makes good soil for a few years, but eventually the nutrients needed by the crops run out and so the farmers often begin to clear more forest.

Above: If logging is done properly, it can make enough money to pay to protect the rest of the rainforest. Only selected trees are cut down and they are removed without damaging younger growth. Forests can be used to grow crops, such as coffee and nuts, without cutting down all the trees.

protected areas are in North America and Europe, where it is illegal to ruin areas of forest wilderness and wetland. Consequently, these places have become wildlife havens. Other protected areas include semi-natural landscapes which double as beauty spots and tourist attractions. Although these areas often have to be extensively altered and managed to meet the needs of the visitors, most still support wildlife communities.

In the developing world, wildlife refuges are a newer phenomenon. Huge areas of Africa's savannahs are protected and populated with many amazing animals. However, the enormous size of these parks makes it very hard to protect the animals, especially elephants and rhinoceroses, from poachers.

Reintroduction

Large areas of tropical forests are now protected in countries such as Brazil and Costa Rica, but often conservation efforts come too late because many animals have either become rare or are completely absent after years of human

Zoo animals

Once zoos were places where exotic animals were merely put on display. Such establishments were increasingly regarded as cruel. Today, the world's best zoos are an integral part of conservation. Several animals, which are classified as extinct in the wild, can only be found in zoos where they are being bred. These breeding programmes are heavily controlled to make sure that closely related animals do not breed with each other. Later, individual animals may be sent around the world to mate in different zoos to avoid in-breeding.

Below: Many of the world's rarest species are kept in zoos, partly so that people can see them, since they are too rare to be spotted in the wild. Giraffes are just one example of the many animals that have been bred successfully in zoos.

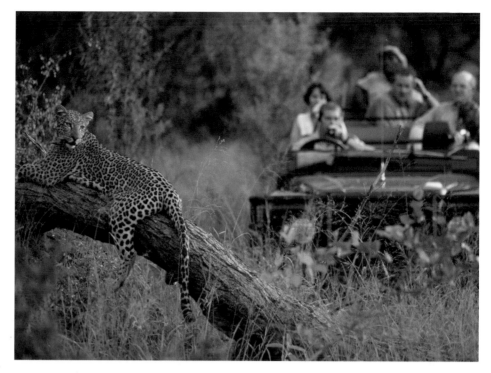

Above: Tourism, such as safaris, is one of the best ways of ensuring that rare animals have somewhere to live. Tourists coming to see the animals in their natural habitat are paying for the upkeep of the nature reserve. However, too many tourists can cause more damage than they prevent.

damage. However, several conservation programmes have reintroduced animals bred in zoos into the wild.

To reintroduce a group of zoo-bred animals successfully into the wild, conservationists need to know how the animal fits into the habitat and interacts with the other animals living there. In addition, for example when trying to reintroduce orang-utans to the forests of Borneo, people have to teach the young animals how to find food and fend for themselves.

Below: Breeding centres are an important way of increasing the number of rare animals. Most, such as this giant panda centre in China, are in the natural habitat. If the animals kept there are treated properly, they should be able to fend for themselves when released back into the wild.

Understanding habitats

A full understanding of how animals live in the wild is also vitally important when conservationists are working in a habitat that has been damaged by human activity. For example, in areas of rainforest which are being heavily logged, the trees are often divided into isolated islands of growth surrounded by cleared ground. This altered habitat is no good for monkeys, which need large areas of forest to swing through throughout the year. The solution is to plant strips of forest to connect the islands of untouched habitat, creating a continuous mass again.

Another example of beneficial human intervention involves protecting rare frogs in the process of migrating to a breeding pond. If their migration necessitates crossing a busy road, it is likely that many of them will be run over. Conservationists now dig little tunnels under the roads so that the frogs can travel in safety. Similar protection schemes have been set up for hedgehogs and ducks, to allow them safe passageways.

CLASSIFICATION

Scientists classify all living things into categories. Members of each category share features with each other – traits that set them apart from other animals. Over the years, a tree of categories and subcategories has been pieced together, showing how all living things seem to be related to each other.

Taxonomy, the scientific discipline of categorizing organisms, aims to classify and order the millions of animals on Earth so that we can better understand them and their relationship to each other. The Greek philosopher Aristotle was among the first people to do this for animals in the 4th century BC. In the 18th century, Swedish naturalist Carolus Linnaeus formulated the system that we use today.

By the end of the 17th century, naturalists had noticed that many animals seemed to have several close relatives that resembled one another. For example lions, lynxes and domestic cats all seemed more similar to each other than they did to dogs or horses. However, all of these animals shared common features that they did not share with frogs, slugs or wasps.

Linnaeus devised a way of classifying these observations. The system he set up – known as the Linnaean system – orders animals in a hierarchy of divisions. From the largest division to the smallest, this system is as follows: kingdom, phylum, class, order, family, genus, species.

Each species is given a two-word scientific name, derived from Latin and Greek. For example, *Panthera leo* is the scientific name of the lion. The first word is the genus name, while the second is the species name. Therefore *Panthera leo* means the "*leo*" species in the genus "*Panthera*". This system of two-word classification is known as binomial nomenclature.

Below: The lion (Panthera leo) *belongs to the genus* Panthera, *the big cats, to which tigers also belong. All cats are members of the large order of* Carnivora *(carnivores) within the class of* Mammalia *(mammals).*

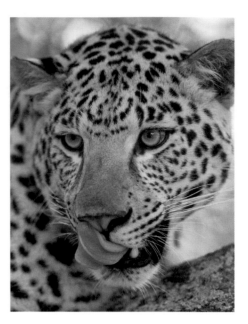

Above: Like the lion, the leopard (Panthera pardus) *belongs to the cat family,* Felidae. *This is divided into two main groups, the big and small cats. The group of small cats includes wildcats and domestic cats.*

Lions, lynxes and other genera of cats belong to the *Felidae* family. The *Felidae* are included in the order *Carnivora*, along with dogs and other similar predators. The *Carnivora*, in turn, belong to the class *Mammalia*, which also includes horses and all other mammals.

Mammals belong to the phylum *Chordata*, the major group which contains all vertebrates, including reptiles, amphibians, birds, fish and some other small animals called tunicates and lancelets. In their turn, *Chordata* belong to the kingdom *Animalia*, comprising around 31 living phyla, including *Mollusca*, which contains the slugs, and *Arthropoda*, which contains wasps and other insects.

Although we still use Linnaean grouping, modern taxonomy is worked out in very different ways from the ones Linnaeus used. Linnaeus and others after him classified animals by their outward appearance. Although they were generally correct when it came

Close relations

Cheetahs, caracals and ocelots all belong to the cat family *Felidae*, which also includes lions, tigers, wildcats, lynxes and jaguars. Although big cats can generally be distinguished from *Felis* by their size, there are exceptions. For example the cheetah is often classed as a big cat, but it is actually smaller than the cougar, a small cat. One of the main behavioural differences between the two groups is that big cats can roar but not purr continuously, while small cats are able to purr but not roar.

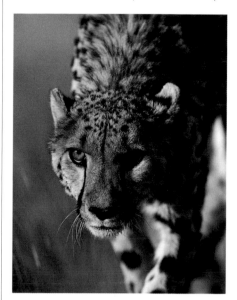

Above: The cheetah (Acinonyx jubatus) *differs from all other cats in possessing retractable claws without sheaths. This species is classed in a group of its own, but is often included within the group of big cats.*

Above: The caracal (Caracal caracal) *is included in the group of small cats, (subfamily* Felinae), *but most scientists place it in a genus of its own,* Caracal, *rather than in the main genus,* Felis.

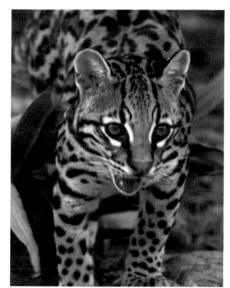

Above: The ocelot (Felis pardalis) *is a medium-sized member of the* Felis *or small cat genus. Like many cats, this species has evolved a spotted coat to provide camouflage unfortunately attractive to hunters.*

Distant relations

All vertebrates (backboned animals) including birds, reptiles and mammals such as seals and dolphins, are thought to have evolved from common fish ancestors that swam in the oceans some 400 million years ago. Later, one group of fish developed limb-like organs and came on to the land, where they slowly evolved into amphibians and later reptiles, which in turn gave rise to mammals. Later, seals and dolphins returned to the oceans and their limbs evolved into paddle-like flippers.

Above: Fish are an ancient group of aquatic animals that mainly propel themselves by thrashing their vertically aligned caudal fin, or tail, and steer using their fins.

Above: In seals, the four limbs have evolved into flippers that make highly effective paddles in water but are less useful on land, where seals are ungainly in their movements.

Above: Whales and dolphins never come on land, and their ancestors' hind limbs have all but disappeared. They resemble fish but the tail is horizontally – not vertically – aligned.

to the large divisions, this method was not foolproof. For example, some early scientists believed that whales and dolphins, with their fins and streamlined bodies, were types of fish and not mammals at all. Today, accurate classification of the various genera is achieved through a field of study called cladistics. This uses genetic analysis to check how animals are related by evolutionary change. So animals are grouped according to how they evolved, with each division sharing a common ancestor somewhere in the past. As the classification of living organims improves, so does our understanding of the evolution of life on Earth and our place within this process.

DIRECTORY OF ANIMALS

Europe and Africa are separated by the Mediterranean Sea, and although the divide is only a few short miles in some places, the two continents are very different, both in terms of climate and their animal life. Europe is not actually a continent at all; it is a large peninsula stretching from the Ural Mountains to the Atlantic Ocean on the western side of the huge Asian landmass. Africa also used to be joined to Asia. It is now cut off entirely by the man-made Suez Canal, but many animals found in Africa also live in parts of Asia. Europe's wildlife might seem ordinary compared to many other parts of the world; many of the animals that once roamed free there, such as lions and bears, are now extinct or at least very rare. Africa, on the other hand, is well known for its wildlife. It is home to the largest land animal of all, the African elephant, as well as the great apes and many other diverse species.

Above from left: Fire salamanders, mandrill, lion.

SALAMANDERS AND RELATIVES

Of the living amphibians, salamanders and newts are the most similar to ancestral amphibians, known from fossils. Salamanders typically have rougher skin than newts and are better able to survive out of water because they have glands to keep their skins moist. They are also frequently brightly coloured and armed with toxins to repel predators.

Olm

Proteus anguinus

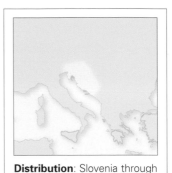

The olm is the world's largest cave-dwelling vertebrate. It lives in the dark, in bodies of cold, underground water. The olm has dull white, sometimes pinkish skin and three tufted, bright red gills on each side of its neck. Its tail is long and eel-like. The olm's gills are filled with blood, allowing the animal to breathe underwater. Oxygen in the water is transferred to the blood via the surface of the gills.

The olm's eyes are reduced to tiny black dots under the skin, leaving it virtually blind. Newly born young have more fully developed eyes than the adults, but these disappear after a year. The olm has a powerful sense of smell and can also find food, communicate and move around by detecting weak electric signals emitted by prey, other olms or inanimate objects such as rocks and pebbles.

Olms have tiny legs for the size of their bodies, with only three stumpy toes on their front legs and two on their back legs. Their snouts are broad and help them to burrow into mud or fine sand to find food, usually freshwater crustaceans.

Olms have elongated bodies, white or pink skin, three pairs of external gills and tiny, skin-covered black eyes that can only perceive light and shadow. Olms were once more common, but numbers have dropped because of water pollution and widespread capture for the pet trade.

Distribution: Slovenia through to Bosnia-Herzegovina.
Habitat: Underground lakes and streams.
Food: Freshwater crustaceans.
Size: 25–30cm (10–12in).
Maturity: Very little information. Thought to be 16–18 years.
Breeding: Females normally give birth to 2 larvae. If the water is warm enough up to 80 eggs may be laid instead.
Life span: 100 years.
Status: Rare.

Fire salamander

Salamandra salamandra

Fire salamanders have poison glands in their skins that are surrounded by special muscles. These are particularly concentrated on their backs. When the muscles contract, they squeeze toxins from the glands. The salamanders can squirt their poison up to 2m (6.5ft). The poison irritates the skin and may affect the nervous systems of any animals that it touches. It can even kill certain predators by paralyzing their lungs, thus stopping them from breathing.

Females are able to store sperm from males for up to two years. They carry 10–40 live young around in their bodies. These are born with their legs well developed, but they still possess larval gills. Some females have been found carrying only four or five young, but these were born fully developed, without gills. By having fewer young, a female is able to provide her offspring with more food. Being so far developed means the young can continue to grow and survive on land, where it is relatively safe.

The fire salamander has a bright yellow and black pattern that warns all would-be predators that it carries toxins. The underside is dark grey with fewer markings. Female fire salamanders are larger than males.

Distribution: Central and southern Europe, Middle East and north-west Africa.
Habitat: Forested, hilly or mountainous country, not far from water.
Food: Invertebrates such as slugs, worms, flies, beetles and centipedes.
Size: 14–17cm (6–7in).
Maturity: Change into adults 2 or 3 months after birth.
Breeding: 10–40 young develop inside female and born after 8 months.
Life span: 20 years.
Status: Common.

Great crested newt

Triturus cristatus

Great crested newts have dark backs, while their bellies are orange or red with large black blotches or spots. The males are more colourful than the females, with tall crests along their backs during the breeding season.

During the breeding season, male great crested newts become brightly coloured, particularly on their bellies. They also develop high toothed crests along their backs and white bands along the sides of their tails. The male newts also have thicker skins than the females at this time.

The newts hibernate on land during the winter. They return to the water around mid-March, and the males develop their breeding livery two or three weeks later. Once the breeding season is over, their crests and outer skins are absorbed into their bodies. Young great crested newts hatch in water as tadpoles. As they develop, they feed on fish, other tadpoles, worms and aquatic insects. The adults feed on larger prey, including newts, frogs and older tadpoles. They locate their prey in the mud at the bottom of their pond, using smell and sight.

Great crested newts are afforded protection by their skins. If threatened, their skins release a white, creamy fluid which is an irritant to the eyes, nose and mouth of predators.

Distribution: England, Scotland, central Europe from France to Urals, and southern Scandinavia to Alps.
Habitat: Spend most of the year in weedy ponds.
Food: Small aquatic invertebrates and vertebrates, including other amphibians.
Size: 11–16cm (4.5–6.5in).
Maturity: Tadpoles change into newts after 8–16 weeks. Reach adult size after 2 years.
Breeding: 200–300 eggs laid between April and mid-July.
Life span: 27 years.
Status: Vulnerable.

Palmate newt (*Triturus helveticus*): 9cm (3.5in)
The palmate newt lives in western Europe, from Scotland to north-west Spain and Portugal. The males have webbed feet, yellow bellies and thin filaments of skin that extend 5mm (0.2in) from the tips of their tails. The females are much duller and lack the tail filaments. They hibernate under logs and stones from November through to March, when they return to water to breed and spend the summer months.

Spectacled salamander (*Salamandrina terdigitata*): 10cm (4in)
The spectacled salamander is found in Italy. It is the only European salamander to have four toes on all four feet. Most others have four on their front feet and five on their back feet. The females are able to store sperm from the males, enabling them to produce young as soon as spring arrives, giving them the best chance of survival. They find mates when there is more time later in the year, and so prepare for the following season.

Marbled newt (*Triturus marmoratus*): 9–11cm (3.5–4.5in)
The marbled newt is found in south-west France, Spain and Portugal. It has a green back, interrupted by a black marbling effect and a grey belly. Both males and females develop orange-red stripes along their backs, from neck to tail. The females keep this stripe when they return to water to breed. During this time, the males lose their red stripes and develop crests, along with silver bands on their tails. When threatened, their tails are erected and swayed from side to side.

Sharp-ribbed newt

Pleurodeles waltl

The sharp-ribbed newt has special rib bones that are able to inject poison into a predator by protruding through special pores in its skin. When the poison enters the skin of a predator, it causes a great deal of pain. The newt will also head-butt a predator, exposing glands at the back of its head that exude a toxic fluid. It has similar glands on its tail, which it lashes to release the toxin.

This species lives permanently in water and will only leave a pool if the water level begins to fall. The newts have flattened bodies to help them slip under rocks and logs. Sharp-ribbed newts breed twice in a year, in early spring and again in midsummer. The males have much longer tails than the females, and during the mating season they develop special pads under their front legs to help grasp the females when transferring sperm.

Distribution: Spain, Portugal and Morocco.
Habitat: Entirely aquatic, in standing water such as ponds, lagoons, dams and irrigation systems.
Food: Invertebrates, small fish and carrion.
Size: 15–30cm (6–12in).
Maturity: 4 years.
Breeding: Female lays between 100 and 1,000 eggs depending on her size. Breeding takes place twice: once in the spring and again in midsummer.
Life span: Not known.
Status: Common.

The sharp-ribbed newt has a dark brown back. Along its sides it has dark blotches with lines of dull orange circles. These are the pores from which the ribs can protrude from its body. Its belly is generally much paler in colour.

FROGS AND TOADS

Throughout the world, there are over 4,000 species of frog and toad – more than ten times the number of salamanders and newts. Frogs are often recognized by their long legs, hopping motion and smooth, often brightly coloured skins. Toads, on the other hand, are often dark brown, warty amphibians that walk rather than hop. However, many frogs and toads are difficult to distinguish from one another.

African clawed toad

Xenopus laevis

Distribution: Southern Africa.
Habitat: Muddy pools.
Food: Small worms, crustaceans, fly larvae and tadpoles of own species.
Size: 6–9cm (2.5–3.5in).
Maturity: Females 15–18 months; males 12 months.
Breeding: Spawn from August–December.
Life span: Over 20 years.
Status: Common.

Today, chemical tests are used to tell whether women are pregnant. However, African clawed toads were once commonly used in hospitals as pregnancy tests. Pregnant women produce a particular hormone, which is released into their urine. If this hormone is present in the urine when injected into female toads, then the toads spontaneously lay eggs. In nature, eggs are laid singly and may be attached to water plants or rocks.

From the head along the toad's sides there are a few rows of small stitch-like lines. Each line is a little depression containing minute hairs that detect vibrations in the water. This helps to tell the toad where it is, the location of other toads or predators, and occasionally food.

African clawed toads like to hang just below the water surface, waiting for food to swim by. They are the only South African amphibians to feed and breed in the water for their whole lives. If their pools dry up, they bury themselves in the mud and wait for the rainy season to arrive.

The African clawed toad is very flat, with small upward-facing eyes. Its skin is very slimy and generally coloured brown, green or grey, with darker spots or blotches on its back. Its belly is a yellowish-white colour.

Cape ghost frog

Heleophryne purcelli

The Cape ghost frog is a small frog with dull green skin, covered in black-brown spots bordered with yellow. Its eyes are a coppery colour.

Cape ghost frogs live in very fast-flowing mountain streams. They have well developed toe pads for clinging to wet rocks in these torrential habitats. Their large hind feet are also webbed, to help them swim against the current. Male Cape ghost frogs also have pads along the insides of their front legs and, prior to the mating season, they develop small spines around the rims of their lower jaws. These modifications help them grasp females and prevent them from being washed away while mating.

The females lay their large eggs under stones or in gravel in shallow backwaters, alongside the main channels of streams. Their tadpoles are long and flat. They, too, must cling on to rocks to avoid being washed away by the torrents. They attach themselves to smooth rocks with their large sucker-like mouths. The tadpoles feed on microscopic algae that grow on the surfaces of the rocks. They use their long, muscular tails to fight against the currents for periods while grazing.

Distribution: South Africa.
Habitat: Fast-flowing streams in mountain areas.
Food: Algae.
Size: 3.5–5cm (1.5–2in).
Maturity: 2 years.
Breeding: Summer.
Life span: Not known.
Status: Common.

Tomato frog (*Dyscophus antongilii*): 5–10cm (2–4in)
Tomato frogs have orange-red backs, yellowish undersides, green eyes and sometimes black spots on their throats. The females are a brighter red than the males. They live in the lowlands of Madagascar, in swamps and shallow pools. Breeding occurs during the rainy season in stagnant or very slow-moving water. Females lay 1,000–1,500 small black and white eggs on the water's surface. The tadpoles are very quick to hatch and do so only 36 hours later, changing into adults after about 45 days.

Mountain ghost frog (*Heleophryne rosei*): 3.5–5cm (1.5–2in)
The mountain ghost frog is extremely rare and restricted to an area only 7–8sq km (1.5sq miles) in size on Table Mountain in South Africa. It has specific breeding requirements and needs areas that have water all year round. The tadpoles take a long time to grow and need at least two seasons before they change into adults.

African "hairy" frog (*Trichobatrachus robustus*): Length not known
The African "hairy" frog lives in western Africa. It gets its name from special hair-like filaments that develop on the male frog's legs and sides. The filaments are full of blood vessels and grow when the frog needs more oxygen to breathe. The species has lungs that are much smaller than the lungs of other frogs of a similar size. This means that when the males become very active as they jostle over females to mate with, they require more oxygen. The filaments act as external lungs, providing them with extra oxygen.

African bullfrog

Pyxicephalus adspersus

To avoid drying up, the African bullfrog can wrap itself in a cocoon. This is made from many layers of dead skin, and looks like plastic film. The frog can survive in this cocoon for two or three months, getting all the moisture it needs by absorbing water from its bladder. When the rains finally arrive, the cocoon softens and splits open. The frog scrambles out and eats the cocoon.

The male guards its eggs and tadpoles in a shallow puddle. Sharp upper teeth and two horny spikes at the tip of the lower jaw help ward off intruders. If the puddle is in danger of drying out, the male digs an escape channel for transferring the tadpoles to water. When the tadpoles develop, they can be aggressive and cannibalistic.

Distribution: Tropical areas across central Africa.
Habitat: Temporary bodies of water and small lakes in open or bush country.
Food: Insects and other invertebrates, reptiles, amphibians, birds and rodents.
Size: Up to 20cm (8in); 2kg (4.5lb).
Maturity: 1–2 years.
Breeding: Female lays up to 4,000 eggs in temporary pools. Tadpoles change into striped froglets but lose their stripes over time.
Life span: More than 20 years.
Status: Not known.

African bullfrogs are generally olive green, with lighter coloured throats and bellies to help them blend in with their surroundings. Juveniles have obvious stripes, which later fade as they get older.

Goliath bullfrog

Conraua goliath

Goliath bullfrogs are the largest frogs in the world, and can grow to more than 30cm (12in) in length. They live in only a few rivers in western Africa and are at risk from disappearing altogether because the rainforests where they live are being cleared for growing crops and grazing cattle. The construction of human settlements and dams built across rivers are also problems for the species because they destroy even more of their habitat.

Adult Goliath bullfrogs eat insects, crustaceans, fish and other amphibians, including newts, salamanders and smaller frogs. Their tadpoles, however, are plant-eaters and will only feed on certain species of water plant that are found near waterfalls and rapids in particular areas. The distribution of the water plants restricts the Goliath bullfrogs to a relatively small region of West Africa.

The Goliath bullfrog is silent, not having a vocal sac in its throat to make any sound. It is a shy species that is hunted by one local forest tribe, who eat them and keep the thigh bones as good-luck charms.

The Goliath bullfrog is a very dark coloured frog, mainly a blackish-green. The belly is a lighter pinkish-orange and the eyes are a coppery brown.

Distribution: Cameroon and Equatorial Guinea.
Habitat: Swiftly flowing rivers in dense rainforests.
Food: Small freshwater invertebrates, fish and other amphibians. Tadpoles eat plants.
Size: 30cm (12in); 3.3kg (7.25lb).
Maturity: Not known.
Breeding: Not known.
Life span: Not known.
Status: Vulnerable.

Common toad

Bufo bufo

The common toad often lives in very dry areas over most of the year. Its thick, loose skin and nocturnal habits help to protect it from drying out. Toads are eaten less commonly than frogs because of foul-tasting chemicals released by glands in their skins. If threatened, the common toad will also inflate its body and rise up on its legs, looking two or three times as big and more intimidating than usual.

Toads are particularly fond of ants, and use their sticky tongues to reach out and catch them. They have a good sense of smell, and this is thought to be very important in helping them to move long distances and find their breeding sites each year. They tend to come out of hibernation during February and March – usually a few weeks later than common frogs.

Rather than laying clumps of spawn, as frogs do, common toads release a long double strand of spawn that becomes entangled in pondweed and other vegetation. In warm weather, tadpoles metamorphose in about eight weeks.

Common toads are olive brown and covered in warts. They have copper-coloured eyes and walk rather than hop like frogs. The males are smaller and have fewer warts than the females, and only the males croak.

Distribution: Most of Europe, north-west Africa, Asia and parts of Oceania.
Habitat: Damp areas of deciduous woodland, scrub, gardens, parks and fields. In the breeding season, they live in ponds, lakes, ditches and slow-moving rivers.
Food: Insects and their larvae, spiders, slugs and worms. Larger toads sometimes prey on slow worms, small grass snakes and harvest mice, which are swallowed alive.
Size: 8–15cm (3–6in).
Maturity: 4 years.
Breeding: 600–4,000 eggs laid.
Life span: 40 years.
Status: Common.

European common frog

Rana temporaria

European common frogs are found in a variety of habitats, including fields and woodland close to water. Their diet is eclectic, including insects, molluscs and worms. Male common frogs have swellings on their first fingers to help them grasp the females when mating. Sometimes two or three males may try to mate with one female. Occasionally she will die in this situation through drowning or being squashed by their combined weight.

Spawning can take place as early as December or January but it is more usual in late February, March or April. Frogs flock to a traditional pond, lake or ditch, where hundreds or thousands may be swimming around. Males emit quiet croaks and can be seen jostling for the best females. While a female is releasing her 1,000–4,000 eggs, the male, directly on top, will spread his sperm over all them.

After spawning, the ponds become quiet again, as the frogs leave to live on land. They do so until the autumn, when they hibernate under logs and rocks. When it is very cold, they will rest in the water, usually in amongst thick vegetation.

Common frogs are variable in colour, but generally have a greenish-brown body colour with darker blotches and dark masks on their faces.

Distribution: Widespread throughout Europe, including Turkey and Russia.
Habitat: Live in meadows, gardens and woodland. Breed in puddles, ponds, lakes and canals. Prefer areas of shallow water.
Food: Insects, snails, slugs and worms, caught with long, sticky tongues. Tadpoles are herbivorous and feed on algae.
Size: 6–10cm (2.5–4in).
Maturity: 3 years.
Breeding: 1,000–4,000 eggs laid.
Life span: 12 years.
Status: Common in most of range.

European tree frog

Hyla arborea

European tree frogs are bright green frogs. They are able to change colour, and when they first come out from hibernation, in the spring, they are grey-brown. They are excellent climbers, living in shrubs and trees throughout southern Europe. They have sucker pads on the ends of their toes to help them grasp branches. The green skin helps to keep them hidden among the leaves.

Tree frogs are most active during the night, particularly if it has been raining. They leap around, catching a variety of night-flying flies and moths. In late spring, the males sit by the edges of ponds or on plants overhanging the water, croaking to attract females. When the males call, they inflate vocal sacs, which produce their distinctive sound. When full of air, the sacs are as big as the frogs. The song produced is similar to the bark of a dog or the quack of a duck. When a number of males croak together throughout the night, they can be heard as far as several kilometres away.

Distribution: Europe, below 800m (2,650ft) above sea level.
Habitat: Scrub and open woodland with shrubs.
Food: Flies and moths.
Size: 3–4.5cm (1.25–2in).
Maturity: Not known.
Breeding: 800–1,000 eggs laid in small clumps during late April or May.
Life span: 20 years.
Status: Declining.

The European tree frog is lime green on top and white underneath. It has a somewhat contorted appearance because the skin on its head is fused to its skull.

Fire-bellied toad (*Bombina bombina*): 3–5cm (1.25–2in)
From above, fire-bellied toads are well camouflaged by their dull, mottled colours. They have black or dark brown warty skins, covered in dark spots with green patches on their shoulders and broad, green central lines. However, the bellies are black with bright red or yellow patches which form a unique pattern, rather like human fingerprints. When adults call, they inflate their throats and show off their bright colours.

Marsh frog (*Rana ridibunda*): Females 7.5–14cm (3–5.5in); males 6.5–10cm (2.5–4in)
The marsh frog lives on the plains and rivers of eastern Europe. It also occurs in western Europe, originally introduced by humans. Its loud croaking can be heard from pools during the day and night. When calling, special sacs are inflated and bulge out on either side of the head. The frogs make these strange and loud calls to attract mates throughout May and June. It is the largest European frog and usually remains in the water for most of the year.

Natterjack toad (*Bufo calamita*): Females 5–8cm (2–3.25in); males 4–7cm (1.5–3in)
The natterjack toad is found throughout western and central Europe and is the smallest of all European toads. It has dark, warty skin like the common toad and a yellow line all the way from the head to the end of the spine. It tends to spawn in shallow fresh water. During the breeding season, the males develop purple-violet throats. The females' throats remain white. Natterjack toads are thought to be Europe's noisiest toads because the male's croaking can travel for up to 3km (2 miles).

Bushveld rain frog

Breviceps adspersus

The Bushveld rain frog is a rather rotund burrowing frog with a short head and blunt snout. It spends most of its life underground, only coming up to the surface to feed and breed after rains. Its globular shape makes burrowing through soft sandy soil easier, but it also makes mating difficult. To help the male stay on top of the female, he secretes a sticky substance from glands around his rear. This acts like a glue and binds him to his mate.

The fertilized eggs are laid in an underground chamber. When mating and egg-laying is over, the glue either breaks down or the female sheds her skin to release the male. The tadpoles are unable to feed and have to develop into froglets before they have their first meal.

The males attract females by giving short, blurred whistles, which are emitted in a continuous series of single calls. Two or more may call together in a chorus.

Distribution: South Africa and Swaziland, Mozambique, Botswana and Namibia.
Habitat: Hot, dry foothills. Dry bushveld in northern part of South African range. Breeds in open and closed woodland with sandy soils.
Food: Insects.
Size: 3–6cm (1.25–2.5in).
Maturity: Not known.
Breeding: After rains.
Life span: Not known.
Status: Common.

The Bushveld rain frog is brown with rows of light yellow or orange patches along its spine and sides. It also has a broad black stripe from each eye to its armpit and a speckled throat, which may be entirely black in males.

Foam-nesting frog

Chiromantis xerampelina

Foam-nesting frogs are found in tropical and subtropical parts of Africa, where they inhabit trees and shrubs of the savannah. When mating, pairs of foam-nesting frogs produce large amounts of foam in which the eggs are laid. The foam masses are attached to branches, overhanging temporary pools of water. The foam stops the eggs from drying out in the hot climate where the frogs live, and females occasionally remoisten it with water.

The tadpoles hatch after two days and survive in the foam as it dries out. After about a week, when the nests become very crowded, the tadpoles drop from the foam into the water below. In most matings, two or three males will be involved with each female. All the males help in beating mucus to produce the foam nests. Male foam-nesting frogs have large testicles to produce copious amounts of sperm. This increases their chances of success in fertilizing the eggs.

Foam-nesting frogs live in areas that reach high temperatures, and they can be found sitting in direct sunlight. They lose very little water from their bodies and have a special skin that turns white in the sunshine. This stops them from heating up and losing water through evaporation. To avoid overheating, they also produce a watery mucus from glands in their waterproof skins.

The foam-nesting frog is a light-coloured, grainy, pale green frog with light brown lines on its legs and irregular spots across its body. Many individuals are darker with brown areas.

Distribution: Tropical and southern subtropical parts of Africa, in the south and west of these areas.
Habitat: Bushes and trees in African grassland.
Food: Large insects.
Size: 6cm (2.5in).
Maturity: Not known.
Breeding: During the rainy season.
Life span: 2.5 years.
Status: Common.

Midwife toad

Alytes obstetricans

Distribution: West and south-west Europe.
Habitat: Quarries, scree slopes and uncultivated land. Sand dunes and gardens are inhabited in France.
Food: Small insects.
Size: 5cm (2in).
Maturity: 2 years.
Breeding: Female lays several batches of 20–60 eggs in strings between April and June, which are carried on the male's back legs. Tadpoles released into water between 2 and 6 weeks later.
Life span: Not known.
Status: Locally common.

The midwife toad looks very similar to the common toad. However, it has vertical pupils instead of horizontal ones, a more pointed snout, and does not have the protective glands behind the head. Midwife toads are night-active and spend the day hidden in crevices in rocks, under logs or in burrows.

In late spring, the males give out short peeping calls to attract females. Mating occurs on land. As the females produce strings of 20–60 eggs, the males catch them with their legs. They then position the strings of spawn between their thighs and waists. The females play no part in looking after the eggs. The eggs remain embedded in a whitish-yellow mass of mucus that keeps them moist.

The male secretes an antibiotic solution over the eggs to protect them from fungal or bacterial attack. After two to six weeks, the eggs develop into fully formed tadpoles. The males travel to ponds where the young release themselves into the water. Some males attract two or more females, and therefore look after a larger number of eggs.

The midwife toad is dull grey, olive or brown in colour, occasionally with green spots and often with darker markings. The belly is whitish with grey blotches. Females sometimes have red spots running down their flanks. This toad is particularly proficient at leaping.

Red-legged pan frog (*Kassina maculata*): 6.5cm (2.5in)
The red-legged pan frog is grey with black oval spots, outlined with thin, light-coloured lines. The parts of the legs that are less visible, such as the rear and armpits, are bright red with black spots. This species is active at night in the lowlands of eastern Africa. Males congregate to call while floating in the water.

Trilling reed frog (*Hyperolius parkeri*): 2.5cm (1in)
This African tree frog is pale lime green in colour with broad, whitish bands on the sides of its body, running from its snout to its tail. It lives in low-lying grasslands in East Africa, where it is active at night. Males send out high-pitched bird-like trills to attract females. The frogs live in trees, reeds and grasses and breed by ponds, where the females lay their 70–110 eggs on vegetation, usually grasses growing over the water. After hatching, the tadpoles drop into the water to complete their development. This is the only African tree frog where the male is larger than the female.

Common squeaker (*Arthroleptis stenodactylus*): 4.25cm (1.75in)
These frogs live in undisturbed forested areas of the Democratic Republic of the Congo, Kenya and southern Africa. The males call during and shortly after rainfall and are commonly heard throughout the forest floor and on steep slopes. Females are thought to lay their eggs and bury them in moist earth, where they develop and hatch into small froglets. The tadpole stage seems to be missed out completely.

Greater leaf-folding frog
Afrixalus fornasinii

Greater leaf-folding frogs inhabit savannah country in eastern and southern Africa. The female lays her eggs on grass overhanging water. She folds the edges over, gluing them together with secretions from a gland on her rear. These leaf nests protect the eggs from predators and from drying out in the sun.

The eggs are pale in colour, lacking pigment. This is common with frogs and toads that lay their eggs in burrows or fold them in leaves. As they are not exposed, the eggs do not need to be coloured or have disruption patterns to camouflage them and help them blend into the surroundings. When the tadpoles have developed, their leaf nests break up and they fall into water, where they continue their development.

Distribution: Eastern and southern Africa.
Habitat: Grasslands, particularly with large bushes and trees. Also found in coastal lowlands and up to 1,300m (4,300ft) above sea level in Malawi.
Food: Eggs and developing larvae of other frogs that breed earlier.
Size: 3–4cm (1.25–1.5in); weight not known.
Maturity: Not known.
Breeding: 80 pale eggs laid on a grass leaf.
Life span: Not known.
Status: Not known.

Greater leaf-folding frogs have a dark reddish-brown body colour. They have black warts on their backs and broad silver bands running along their sides from their snouts to their rear. These frogs feed on the spawn and tadpoles of other frogs that breed earlier than they do.

Banded rubber frog

Phrynomerus bifasciatus

The banded rubber frog is pear-shaped, with shiny smooth skin. It is nocturnal and breeds early in the season in floodwaters. The males issue melodious trills, lasting several seconds, from the banks or on floating vegetation. The eggs are laid in large masses on the water's surface or attached to aquatic plants.

The frog has a bright black and red skin, signalling to predators that it is poisonous. The skin, which becomes paler in bright light, contains toxins that can harm any animal that attempts to eat it. During the dry season the banded rubber frog seeks cover in tree hollows and burrows, away from the heat and dryness. This species is also known as the African snake-necked frog, because it is able to bend its neck much more than typical frogs.

The banded rubber frog is a shiny black frog with red spots on its legs and thick red bands running from its eyes, right along the sides of its body.

Distribution: South-eastern Africa.
Habitat: Not known.
Food: Insects.
Size: 7.25cm (3in); weight not known.
Maturity: Not known.
Breeding: Spawn laid in water.
Life span: Not known.
Status: Not known.

TURTLES AND TORTOISES

Tortoises, terrapins and turtles appeared on Earth around 200 million years ago. Tortoises are the land form of the three and have dome-shaped shells. Terrapins tend to live in fresh water while turtles live in sea water, although this is not always the case, and both are often grouped as turtles. Terrapins and turtles have flatter shells than tortoises; they also have webbed feet or flippers and are usually carnivores.

European pond turtle

Emys orbicularis

European pond turtles used to be common in Britain when the weather warmed after the last Ice Age, but they disappeared around 5,000 years ago when temperatures fell once more. Today the species is found across the rest of Europe, including northern France. Although the adult turtle can survive the British climate, it is too cool for the eggs to hatch successfully. During warm weather, European pond turtles can be found basking on exposed rocks. They can be quite shy and if disturbed will quickly dive back into the water where their webbed feet allow them to move around rapidly.

Males can mate with females throughout a seven-month period from March to October, although most activity is seen during March and April. Two or three months after mating the females lay 3–16 eggs in burrows. The young turtles hatch in August and September before the onset of autumn and winter.

The European pond turtle has a smooth, oval shell. Younger individuals have lighter, sometimes yellowish, spots and streaks on their shells, necks and heads. Older individuals are entirely dark. They hibernate in winter, burying themselves in mud.

Distribution: Europe, North Africa and western Asia.
Habitat: Ponds, lakes and slow-moving streams.
Food: Fish, amphibians, insects, molluscs, young snakes and small mammals.
Size: 18–35cm (7–14in); 5–10kg (11–22lb). Female larger.
Maturity: Females 15 years; males 12 years.
Breeding: Females lay eggs in soil during June.
Life span: Up to 120 years.
Status: Common.

Leatherback turtle

Dermochelys coriacea

The leatherback turtle is the world's largest marine turtle. Its shell has a leathery texture and is semi-rigid; it is made from thousands of individual tiny bony plates connected together. Each can move a little, making the shell more flexible than if it were completely solid. The turtles have long front flippers that enable them to swim up to 30km (20 miles) per day.

Leatherback turtles are very unusual reptiles because they are able to generate body heat through the movement of their muscles. The heat is maintained by the turtle's huge size, layers of fat under the skin and also by a long oesophagus, which coils back before reaching the stomach, helping to heat up swallowed food.

The turtles also have special blood vessels that stop heat being lost to cold water. Heat is transferred from arteries entering the flippers to veins carrying blood away from the flippers, keeping the limbs colder than the rest of the body. Mating takes place at sea and the females nest on tropical beaches, where they lay eggs in pits dug into sand.

Distribution: Atlantic, Pacific and Indian Oceans.
Habitat: Marine water.
Food: Jellyfish.
Size: 2–3m (6.5–10ft); up to 900kg (1,980lb).
Maturity: 30–50 years.
Breeding: 80–100 eggs laid on beaches every other year, hatching after 60 days.
Life span: Over 50 years.
Status: Critically endangered.

The leatherback turtle has a dark grey or black upper surface with additional spotting. Ridges run from the front end of the shell down to the tail. The span of the flippers is equal to the length of the animal.

Leopard tortoise

Geochelone pardalis

The leopard tortoise is a very distinctive tortoise, with obvious black and yellowish markings on its shell. The shell patterns are extremely variable; indeed each pattern is unique, like human fingerprints. Leopard tortoises from Ethiopia are a pale race, while those from South Africa are exceptionally large.

A musk gland near the tail emits a powerful and distinctive smell, which is used by the tortoises to attract partners for mating or to drive away predators.

When it becomes very hot, the leopard tortoise digs a hole in the soil and remains underground to avoid overheating or dehydrating. It stays in the burrow until the temperatures fall and the rains come again. If food becomes hard to find, the tortoises travel long distances to seek more. To continue growing healthy shells and ensure their bones remain strong, they eat old bones found when they forage.

The leopard tortoise is straw-coloured, with black blotches evenly spread over the shell. Shell markings are reminiscent of the pelt of a leopard cat, hence the tortoise's name.

Distribution: South and east Africa, south of the Sahara.
Habitat: Semi-arid, thorny and dry grassland habitats.
Food: Grasses, fruit of the prickly pear, thistles and other plants.
Size: 40–65cm (16–26in); 10–40kg (22–88lb).
Maturity: 6–10 years.
Breeding: Eggs laid in autumn.
Life span: 50–150 years.
Status: Vulnerable.

Radiated tortoise (*Geochelone radiata*): 40cm (16in)
The radiated tortoise is a very colourful tortoise with streaks radiating out from each section of its shell. It lives on the island of Madagascar and is less common than it used to be because the Chinese prize it as a purported aphrodisiac. The vegetation where it lives is disappearing, including a type of spiny cactus, which provides important cover for the tortoise. Males and females encounter each other during late afternoon sorties, but they only mate if it is dry.

Atlantic or **Kemp's ridley turtle** (*Lepidochelys kempii*): 50–70cm (20–28in)
The Atlantic ridley turtle is the smallest marine turtle and the most endangered. The turtles live in sheltered areas such as large estuaries, bays and lagoons where they feed on crabs, jellyfish, squid, snails, starfish and a variety of other marine invertebrates, as well as some seaweeds. They have distinctive heart-shaped shells that may be black, grey-brown or olive in colour.

East African side-necked turtle (*Pelusios subniger*): 20cm (8in)
The East African side-necked turtle lives in shallow ponds and streams with muddy bottoms. When the pools dry out or it gets too hot or cold, the turtle burrows into the mud and remains protected until the rains come. When threatened, this species pulls its neck to one side rather than bringing it back into the shell like typical tortoises and turtles. They have dark – often black – domed shells with yellow undersides. They are found in East Africa, below the Sahara Desert and throughout Madagascar.

Pancake tortoise

Malacochersus tornieri

The pancake tortoise is very rare and suffered from illegal pet trade in the 1960s and 70s. Its tiny size meant it could be smuggled out of Kenya and Tanzania in very large numbers. The tortoise lives in rocky cliffs, hidden in crevices during the day. Grasses are very important for feeding and breeding. These grassy areas around the cliffs are disappearing through human activity, which prevents the species from increasing its population.

The pancake tortoise has a lightweight shell, which helps it scurry along and escape from predators more quickly. The bony plates that make up the shell are reduced in this species, leaving spaces where the bones would be, making it less heavy and more flexible. The shell is also flattened, which helps the tortoise to rest or escape under very low rocks. The tortoise can wedge itself into crevices by inflating its lungs with air and pushing down with its legs. If the tortoise falls and lands on its back, it can right itself quite easily.

The pancake tortoise has a brown shell, marked with pale yellow and black. It has a more pronounced hook to its beak than other species. The males have longer, thicker tails than the females.

Distribution: Kenya and Tanzania.
Habitat: Small rocky cliffs called "kopjes", over 1,000m (3,280ft) above sea level.
Food: Dry grasses and vegetation.
Size: 15cm (6in).
Maturity: Not known.
Breeding: Single eggs laid 3 or 4 times a year.
Life span: 25 years.
Status: Endangered.

LIZARDS

Of all the reptiles in the world, 80 per cent are lizards and snakes. Lizards are able to move their upper jaws as well as their lower jaws, helping them to tackle large prey and swallow them more easily. Many also possess the ability to lose their tails if attacked by predators; special bones in the tail are pulled apart by muscles and the tail is released from the body. This is called autotomy.

Panther chameleon

Furcifer pardalis

Throughout the range of the panther chameleon, males and females vary in colour. There are at least 25 different forms, with each one occurring in a different region. Males from north-west Madagascar are bright turquoise and green, with red and gold colours radiating from their eyes and heads. Another type of male from a different region has up to six different body colours with white streaks around its eyes. Breeding females become brighter too, developing black and red-orange colouring. Their black markings vary in pattern. The panther chameleon is able to change colour very quickly when it moves into different vegetation – as camouflage – or when being approached by other chameleons – as communication. They can be very aggressive with one another, and changing colour can warn other individuals to keep away.

Males have white stripes along their bodies and can display a variety of colours. Females are grey or brown, but turn red-orange when breeding.

Distribution: North and east Madagascar. Introduced to Reunion and Mauritius and neighbouring islands.
Habitat: Lowland coastal areas.
Food: Small insects.
Size: Females 18–23cm (7–9in); males: 30–45cm (12–18in). Weight not known.
Maturity: Females 5 months; males 12 months.
Breeding: 4–6 clutches of 12–30 eggs are laid per year.
Life span: Not known.
Status: Vulnerable.

Armadillo lizard

Cordylus cataphractus

The armadillo lizard lives in groups of up to 30 animals. Small groups, with nine lizards or fewer, are usually all females with just one adult male. Larger groups contain more males. They are active during the day, searching for insects in the dry desert areas in which they live. Their sandy colour keeps them hidden from birds and other reptiles, and their spines act as a protective armour.

If they are out in the open, away from cover, and are threatened by a predator, armadillo lizards will roll themselves into balls like armadillos, keeping a tight hold of their tails with their mouths. This exposes their tough, horny skin and spines, making it difficult for a predator to eat the lizard. If the lizard has enough time, or is close to cover, it will squeeze into a small crevice in nearby rocks. Because it has a flattened body, few predators are able to follow it into its hideaway.

Armadillo lizards have flattened bodies and broad heads. The body is sandy yellow or brown and covered with spiny scales. They have either yellow or violet throats, embellished with brown blotches. When threatened, these lizards roll into a tight ball, creating a spiny ring.

Distribution: Southern tip of Africa.
Habitat: Dry, desert areas with plants able to withstand drought and high temperatures.
Food: Insects, spiders and other invertebrates.
Size: 7.5–16.5cm (3–6.5in); 400–800g (0.9–1.75lb).
Maturity: Not known.
Breeding: Females give birth to 1 or 2 young lizards towards the end of summer.
Life span: Not known.
Status: Uncommon.

Sand lizard (*Lacerta agilis*): 18–19cm (7–7.5in)
The sand lizard is a colourful species found throughout most of Europe and central Asia. During courtship, fighting may occur between males for the biggest and most fertile females. Females lay 4–12 eggs in dry, sandy soil close to vegetation. Males are bright green, while females are generally brown with darker patterning along their bodies.

African plated lizard (*Gerrhosaurus validus*): 69cm (27in)
Plated lizards live on the rocky hills in southern Africa and use the crevices between rocks to hide. During midsummer, four large, oval eggs are laid between rocks and covered with soil. Plated lizards are dark brown or black, with yellow spots and shields on their heads. Their throats are whitish and their bellies are light brown. Males develop a pinkish-purple hue on their throats, chins and the sides of their heads during the breeding season.

Fat-tailed gecko (*Hemitheconyx caudicinctus*): Females 20cm (8in); males 25cm (10in)
Fat-tailed geckos are very striking in appearance, with alternating thick bands of colour. These are dark brown combined with lighter brown, orange-brown or pinkish-brown. Their bellies are pale pink or white. They live in dry grassland and woodland in western Africa, appearing at night to feed on small insects. If the lizard regrows its tail following an attack, the tail will be much shorter and fatter than before, resembling its head. This is a defence mechanism, designed to fool predators into attacking the wrong end.

Slow worm

Anguis fragilis

The slow worm has a long, smooth body and lacks legs. Although it is often mistaken for a snake, it is a legless lizard. Unlike snakes, it has moveable eyelids so that it can blink. It also has a broader, flatter tongue with a notch at the tip rather than a deep fork.

Slow worms hibernate between October and March. The males appear before the females, and when they come out in the spring, they warm themselves up by resting under rocks and logs. Slow worms are secretive creatures and spend most of their time underground. If they are picked up, they will shed their tails, which continue to wriggle for about 15 minutes. This distracts a predator while the slow worm escapes.

Distribution: Europe, South-west Asia and western Siberia.
Habitat: Rough grassland, hedgerows, heathland, woodland edges, downs and moorland. Also found in gardens and along railway or motorway embankments.
Food: Molluscs and earthworms, and also insects and spiders.
Size: 30–50cm (12–20in).
Maturity: Females 4–5 years; males 3–4 years.
Breeding: Mate in summer; eggs incubated inside body.
Life span: 10–15 years.
Status: Common.

Females are brown with coppery or reddish-coloured backs. Dark stripes run down each side of the body. Males are brown and lack the dark stripes. Both sexes have whitish or reddish bellies and throats, with copper-red eyes.

Savannah monitor

Varanus albigularis

The savannah monitor lizard is a large lizard with a sandy coloured skin, patterned with lines of small black spots. The amount of black can vary and may be quite extensive. The head is darker on top and the tail has black bands. These lizards inhabit dry savannah or rocky terrain, and feed mostly on invertebrates.

The savannah monitor lives in very hot, grassy habitats, feeding on small mammals and insects. During the breeding season, males will search for females. In the Namib Desert, they have been known to travel up to 6km (3.5 miles) per day looking for females ready to mate. Their territories may be up to 18sq km (7sq miles) in size. Females ready to breed will climb trees to make themselves more obvious to males, and release a pheromone into the air.

During very hot weather, savannah monitors help to keep themselves cool by sitting with their mouths open and vibrating their throats very quickly. This is known as gular fluttering and allows water to evaporate from the throat, thus cooling the blood passing through this area. They are unable to sweat, and their covering of tough, waterproof scales means they can lose little heat through their skin.

Distribution: Eastern and southern Africa.
Habitat: Dry grassland or rocky areas.
Food: Mainly invertebrates plus reptiles, birds, mammals, eggs and carrion.
Size: 1–1.9m (3.25–6.25ft); 6–10kg (13–22lb).
Maturity: 2 years.
Breeding: Up to 50–60 eggs laid in burrows during the spring.
Life span: Not known.
Status: Vulnerable.

Viviparous lizard

Lacerta vivipara

One of the most common European reptiles, the viviparous lizard is found across northern and central Europe and into northern parts of Asia. It is the only reptile found in Ireland. This indicates that it was the fastest reptile to broaden its range back northwards when temperatures increased following the last Ice Age, reaching Ireland before the Irish Sea rose up and engulfed the land-bridge connecting it with mainland Britain and the rest of Europe.

Viviparous means "live birth" – viviparous lizards don't lay eggs, but give birth to fully formed young. These miniatures of their parents are completely independent from birth, receiving no help from their mothers. However, by keeping the eggs within their bodies until they have hatched, the female viviparous lizards have already given their progeny a head-start, since they don't have to lie prone and defenceless as eggs.

The viviparous lizard is a common sight in the UK, for those that look closely enough. Up close they are striking animals, with delicate patterns of coloured scales. However, from a distance they blend easily into the background, making life difficult for kestrels and other predators.

The skin of the viviparous lizard is patterned with a mosaic of brown, dark-green and bronze scales.

Distribution: Northern and central Europe and northern Asia.
Habitat: Wide-ranging habitats including woodland, marshland, heath, sand dunes, hedgerows, bogs and rubbish dumps.
Food: Insects, spiders, snails and earthworms.
Size: 10–16cm (4–6.5in).
Maturity: Not known
Breeding: 3–10 live young born between June and September.
Life span: 8 years
Status: Common.

European glass lizard

Ophisaurus apodus

Distribution: South-east Europe and south-west Asia.
Habitat: Open woodland and fields.
Food: Molluscs, insects and small vertebrates.
Size: Up to 1.2m (4ft).
Maturity: 2–3 years.
Breeding: 8–10 eggs.
Life span: 60 years.
Status: Common.

European glass lizards belong to a family of lizards that have given up the pedestrian way of life, preferring instead to crawl around on their bellies in the manner of snakes. Indeed, having lost their legs almost entirely, glass lizards are often mistaken for snakes. Nevertheless, they can be identified as lizards due to their having ears and eyelids, features which snakes do not possess.

A glass lizard's body also differs from that of a snake by the length of its tail. The tail of a snake – the portion of the body behind the anus and genitals – usually only makes up a small proportion of its body length, whereas two-thirds of a glass lizard's body is made up of tail. The tail also gives rise to the glass lizard's name. Like other lizards, this species is able to shed its tail when threatened – a process called autotomy. However, unlike those of other lizards, the glass lizard's tail then breaks up into lots of small pieces, as though it were shattering like glass. As the actual body of the snake is not much bigger than one of the pieces of tail, people used to believe that these lizards were entirely made from glass.

Not a snake but a lizard with no legs, the European glass lizard has a groove down each side of its body. These legless reptiles are fairly common in fields and highly wooded areas, where they hunt hard-shelled snails and insects.

African fire skink

Lygosoma fernandi

The African fire skink is a medium-sized member of the varied and widespread skink family. It is also one of the most spectacular-looking members of that group. When not in breeding coloration, the male's sides are bright red, merging into the copper colour on its back. This is very impressive in its own right. However, come the breeding season, the red colours extend up on to the back, becoming suffused with the copper and resulting in a brilliant orange. Meanwhile, both pairs of legs darken to near black, with a few light spots, and pearlescent stripes extend from the throat right down the lizard's body. Even juveniles are brightly coloured, having intense light blue tails, which slowly fade as they grow older.

Adult fire skinks are territorial, defending their burrows in the leaf litter on the forest floor from invaders. Their bright colours make them highly visible to predators, so they really need handy bolt-holes for when trouble appears.

The fire skink really lives up to its name, with its shiny scales of many colours – from black and blue to red and gold, including stripes that look like fire on their sides. These fiercely territorial lizards dart among the dead leaves of the forest floor, looking like living flames.

Distribution: West Africa.
Habitat: Tropical forest.
Food: Invertebrates.
Size: 30cm (12in).
Maturity: 1 year.
Breeding: Female fire skinks lay 6 clutches of 4–9 eggs per year.
Life span: 10 years.
Status: Threatened.

Ibiza wall lizard (*Podarcis pityusensis*): 20cm (8in)
Native to the Balearic Islands, this is a slim, agile and very hardy lizard, mainly inhabiting barren, sun-baked rocks, often by the seashore. It can also be found combing neglected gardens, rubbish dumps and wasteground for scraps to complement its usual diet of insects and some plant matter. The colouring of this lizard is variable but there seem to be two predominant forms: those from Formentera have green backs with grey-brown sides, while those from Ibiza have brown backs and reddish sides.

Hierro giant lizard (*Gallotia simonyi*): 60cm (24in)
Once believed to be extinct but rediscovered in 1975, the Hierro giant lizard has at present only a small population of 150 individuals, living on the island of El Hierro in the Canary Islands. It is Europe's most endangered reptile. A herbivorous lizard, it feeds almost exclusively on only two types of plant. It is a stocky lizard with a broad head and pronounced jowls. The giant lizard is very shy, and has not coped well with the expansion of tourism in the Canary Islands.

Hardun (*Laudakia stellio*): 20–30cm (8–12in)
A lizard of many names, the hardun is also known as the starred agama, painted dragon and sling-tailed agama. It is found in Greece, south-west Asia and north-east Africa. Like many agamas, harduns can change colour to express their moods. They bask on stone walls, rocks and buildings, and also on trees. They are usually found in rocky habitats, and are quite shy, being very ready to dive into cracks to hide from potential predators.

Moorish gecko

Tarentola mauritanica

Moorish geckos are Europe's most common geckos. They are also found throughout North Africa. Like many of the world's most successful animals, they have learned to live alongside people and even benefit from their presence. They spend most of their time literally hanging around houses. Geckos are fantastic climbers, even able to climb up panes of glass and hang from ceilings. They are able to do this thanks to their toes, which have many tiny suction pads on their undersides. The pads actually comprise thousands of micro-hairs, which form a temporary molecular bond with the surface being walked over.

Moorish geckos are usually easy to spot, since they tend to congregate at night around wall lights. They do this to wait for their favourite food – moths – to arrive. As the moths are drawn in by the light, they become easy prey for the geckos.

Geckos are the only lizards to possess voiceboxes, which allow them to produce the "gecko" calls from which they get their name. They also produce a "tutting" noise, used between rival males.

The Moorish gecko is also known as the crocodile gecko because of its rough scales.

Distribution: Mediterranean regions.
Habitat: Dry, rocky areas.
Food: Mainly insects.
Size: 15cm (6in).
Maturity: 2 years.
Breeding: Up to 6 clutches of 1–6 eggs per year.
Life span: Not known.
Status: Common, but declining due to collection for the pet trade.

CROCODILES

The last living members of an ancient group known as the archosaurs, crocodiles are little changed from the days of the dinosaurs. The 25 surviving species stand as testament to the success of the crocodilian body design. Thick, scaly skin keeps predators at bay, a special respiratory system allows them to keep hidden underwater for up to five hours at a time, and powerful jaws make them fearsome predators.

Nile crocodile

Crocodylus niloticus

Nile crocodiles were once widespread in eastern and southern Africa, but are now scarcer. With powerful jaws, strong tails, a terrifying turn of speed and stealth belying their enormous size, these crocodiles are efficient killing machines. Nile crocodiles have evolved to be very good at fishing, and during the times of the year when fish migrate along the rivers, they hunt cooperatively. Forming cordons across rivers, they herd the fish into shallow waters, where they can be picked off with ease.

Nile crocodiles are ecologically important as predators. They help to keep the environment in balance by eating catfish, which are predators themselves. By keeping the catfish numbers in check, Nile crocodiles allow the smaller fish, which are eaten by catfish, to thrive, providing food for more than 40 species of bird. In turn, bird droppings fertilize the waters, keeping them rich enough to support a large diversity of life.

The Nile crocodile's powerful body is covered in greyish plate-like scales. The powerful tail is ridged with two keels of scales.

Distribution: Africa (not in the north-west or Sahara region) and Madagascar.
Habitat: Rivers, freshwater marshes, estuaries and mangrove swamps.
Food: Fish, water birds and land mammals.
Size: 3.5–6m (11.5–20ft); up to 225kg (495lb).
Maturity: 10 years.
Breeding: 25–100 eggs laid in nest.
Life span: 45 years.
Status: Common.

Dwarf crocodile

Osteolaemus tetraspis

Distribution: West Africa.
Habitat: Freshwater lakes, swamps and slow-moving rivers.
Food: Fish, birds, crustaceans and occasionally small mammals.
Size: 1.8m (6ft).
Maturity: 6 years.
Breeding: Clutches of up to 20 eggs.
Life span: 40 years.
Status: Vulnerable.

Like other crocodilians, female dwarf crocodiles make very attentive mothers. Laying their eggs in mounds of rotting vegetation on the shore, the females guard them fiercely for the three months it takes for them to incubate. As hatching time arrives, they dig the eggs out of the nests to help the hatchlings escape. They may even roll the eggs gently around in their mouth to break the shells open.

Once out of their eggs, the young face a journey fraught with danger down to the water, but the mothers are there to help again. With surprising gentleness, they pick up their babies in their mouths and flip them into their throat pouches, before carrying them down to the water.

Although adapted to life in water, dwarf crocodiles, like most crocodilians, make shelters on land. These are underground dens dug into the banks of rivers and lakes. They are connected to the outside world by entrances and exit tunnels, both of which can be several metres (tens of feet) long.

Dwarf crocodiles are also known as broad-fronted crocodiles, because of their broad, blunt snouts. People once thought they were cannibals because they carry their young in their mouths.

SNAKES

Snakes are unable to chew their food, so they have to be able to swallow it whole. They are capable of eating large prey items thanks to their perfectly adapted jaws, which they are able to dislocate at will. By detaching their lower jaws from their upper jaws, the snakes are able to open their mouths around animals that are larger than their own heads.

Boomslang

Dispholidus typus

Distribution: Southern Africa.
Habitat: Open woodland.
Food: Reptiles, mammals and birds.
Size: 1.3m–2m (4.25–6.5ft)
Maturity: Not known.
Breeding: 8–13 eggs laid in early summer.
Life span: 18 years.
Status: Common.

Weight for weight, the venom produced by the boomslang is more potent than that of either mambas or cobras. However, the boomslang's shy nature has led to it having less of a fearful reputation than its better-known relatives. Boomslangs also lack the large front fangs of mambas and cobras, having small teeth located at the backs of their mouths. To inject a large amount of poison, boomslangs have to deliver more prolonged bites than front-fanged snakes.

The word boomslang means "tree snake" in Afrikaans – the colonial language of South Africa. This name is very apt, since they are very agile snakes that can slide gracefully through the branches of trees, helped by their strong prehensile tails. Nevertheless, while hunting they will come down to the ground on a fairly regular basis in search of prey.

Most of a boomslang's life is spent coiled and immobile among branches. So effective is their camouflage that birds, which make up a substantial part of the their diet, have been known to actually perch on them.

When immobile in trees, boomslangs are very hard to spot. Their green bodies blend perfectly with the foliage. These highly venomous snakes are members of the colubrid snake family, unlike mambas and cobras.

Common egg-eating snake

Dasypeltis scabra

Very few other snakes share the dietary habits of this fascinating species. Generally most active at night, egg-eating snakes hide out during the day in sheltered areas under rocks or logs. During the night they mainly prey on the eggs of weaverbirds. They are very adept at climbing trees to get to their nests. The snakes test the eggs with their tongues to check whether they have gone off or not. This is important because they cannot spit rotten eggs out once they have swallowed them.

Having found a fresh egg, a snake holds it tightly between its coils and slowly pushes its mouth over and around it. Once the egg is inside the snake's body, it passes farther down the throat until it meets a series of tooth-like structures attached to the vertebrae. These pierce the egg when the snake makes a series of sharp sideways movements of its head. The contents of the egg then drain out of the shell to be digested. Once empty, the egg shell is crushed up and regurgitated from the body. This ability to deal with shells is rare among snakes.

Egg-eating snakes can swallow eggs up to three times the size of their own heads.

Distribution: Southern and central parts of Africa, south of the Sahara Desert.
Habitat: Lowland evergreen forest.
Food: Birds' eggs.
Size: 50–90cm (20–36in).
Maturity: Not known.
Breeding: 6–25 eggs laid each year.
Life span: 14 years.
Status: Common.

Grass snake

Natrix natrix

Grass snakes have dark green bodies with black flecking and whitish-yellow collars around their necks. They inhabit Britain as far as the Scottish border counties.

The grass snake is the most common snake in the Britain. It owes its success to its versatility, being able to hunt both on land and in the water. It prefers to prey on frogs, toads and fish, when it can. To acquire enough heat to be able to function properly, the grass snake has to spend much of its time basking in sunlight. However, this does leave it rather exposed to attack from birds of prey. Foxes, badgers and hedgehogs will also make a meal out of it if they get the chance, but this isn't easy. When threatened, a grass snake has a range of defensive tactics including loud hissing, inflating its body with air, biting, producing a foul-smelling secretion from its anus and playing dead.

Not only is keeping warm a problem for adult grass snakes, it is a problem for the eggs, too. If they are too cold they will take too long to develop, or not hatch at all. Female grass snakes combat this problem by travelling large distances to find suitable places to lay them. Heaps of rotting vegetation, such as compost heaps, are favoured.

Distribution: Europe from Scandinavia south to the Mediterranean, north Africa and central Asia east to Lake Baikal, Russia.
Habitat: Prefer damp grasslands, ditches and river banks.
Food: Amphibians, fish, small mammals and small birds.
Size: 0.7–2m (2.25–6.5ft).
Maturity: Not known.
Breeding: 8–40 eggs laid in June, July or August depending on the latitude, about 8 weeks after mating.
Life span: 20 years.
Status: Common.

Adder

Vipera berus

The majority of members of the viper family are venomous, and the adder – or common viper – is no exception. However, it poses little threat to humans. Adders rarely bite humans, and even when they do, the consequences are usually no more than a painful swelling around the area of the bite. Adders spend most of their day basking in the sunshine, and go out to hunt in the late afternoon. As winter closes in, adders prepare to hibernate, usually burrowing underground to sleep through the cold weather. The duration of hibernation varies with latitude.

The active periods of adders can be divided into three distinct phases. During spring, they come out of hibernation and disperse. This is when the males, having shed their skins, go in search of females, and mating occurs. With the onset of summer, adders migrate along hedgerows and ditches to prime feeding grounds, such as wet meadows. There they stay until summer starts to draw to a close, when they head back to drier areas. The females give birth to their young – they do not lay eggs – which immediately prepare to hibernate too.

Distribution: Throughout Europe and northern and western Asia.
Habitat: Open places such as heaths, meadows and woodland edges.
Food: Lizards, small mammals, nestlings and insects.
Size: 65cm (26in).
Maturity: Not known.
Breeding: 10 young born in late summer.
Life span: 15 years.
Status: Common.

The adder's predominantly grey-brown colour, with zigzag markings down the back, is very different from the coloration of the grass snake, yet people often confuse the two.

Schlegel's blindsnake

Rhinotyphlops schlegelii

Schlegel's blindsnake has very small eyes that are barely capable of vision. The snake's tiny head is covered by large protective scales called scutes. These are often referred to collectively as the "beak".

Schlegel's blindsnake is exceptionally large, being over twice as long as nearly all other blindsnakes. Blindsnakes spend most of their lives underground. This behaviour has earned them their alternative name: wormsnakes. The subterranean environment they occupy has meant that blindsnakes' eyes are mere vestiges of those of their above-ground relatives. However, like Schlegel's blindsnake, few are completely blind. Schlegel's blindsnake is also typical in that it only has teeth in the upper jaw of its small, blunt head. These are all the teeth it needs, because the blindsnake spends most of its time around ant and termite mounds, where it feasts on the soft bodies of the developing insects. The protective beak over the snake's head helps it to tunnel through soft soil without injury. The snake's long, thin body is also covered in smooth, shiny scales that aid in burrowing. Although they are totally harmless, it is unwise to harass blindsnakes. They have well-developed glands near their anuses, packed full of the most noxious-smelling secretions, which they eject upon attack.

Distribution: Southern Africa from Kenya to South Africa.
Habitat: Soft, sandy or loamy soils.
Food: Pupae, eggs and larvae of ants, termites and other subterranean insects.
Size: 1m (3.25ft).
Maturity: Not known.
Breeding: Lays up to 60 eggs underground, which hatch after 4–6 weeks.
Life span: Not known.
Status: Common.

Smooth snake (*Coronella austriaca*): 60cm (24in)
Smooth snakes are Britain's rarest snakes, restricted to just a handful of sites in southern England. They are not venomous at all, killing small rodents and lizards by constriction. Unlike grass snakes and adders, which have keel-shaped scales, smooth snakes have flat, smooth scales; hence their name.

Montpellier snake (*Malpolon monspessulanus*): 2m (6.5ft)
Very fast and shy, Montpellier snakes will flee at the first sign of a disturbance. They prefer open and dry grassland with stones and slopes exposed to sunlight, where they are active only on warm and sunny days. They feed mainly on lizards, which are hunted by sight.

Hooded snake (*Macroprotodon cucullatus*): 60cm (24in)
A unique member of the snake family, the hooded snake is not a very well-known species. Its habitat is always dry and stony. It preys on lizards, which it attacks while they are sleeping, paralyzing them with a mild venom harmless to people. The hooded snake can move quickly and if surprised it will throw its head back to show its underside before fleeing for shelter.

Leopard snake

Elaphe situla

Lacking any venom worth speaking of, leopard snakes are constrictors – they squeeze their prey to death. While the young feed mainly on small lizards, adults prefer to eat rodents. It is this fondness for rats and mice that has made leopard snakes popular pets in some parts of their range. Active mainly by day, leopard snakes are attracted to human settlements by the abundance of rats and mice to be found there. Indeed, in some parts of Greece, far from being feared, people used to actively introduce these snakes into their homes as a way of controlling pests. They are even considered to be good luck charms by superstitious people.

The leopard snake's good reputation, and its ability to live alongside humans, has played highly in its favour, and it is still a common sight throughout much of its range in south-eastern Europe.

The magnificent leopard snake is easily identified by the striking red markings after which it is named.

Distribution: South-eastern Europe.
Habitat: Dry, rocky slopes.
Food: Small mammals and birds.
Size: 1m (3.25ft).
Maturity: Not known.
Breeding: Clutches of 2–5 eggs laid in July or August.
Life span: 15 years.
Status: Common.

Spitting cobra

Naja pallida

Distribution: Eastern and central Africa from southern Egypt to northern Tanzania.
Habitat: Savannah grasslands.
Food: Amphibians, small mammals, birds, eggs and other reptiles.
Size: 0.7–1.5m (2.25–5ft).
Maturity: Not known.
Breeding: Clutches of up to 15 eggs.
Life span: 20 years.
Status: Common.

As its name indicates, this snake has a particularly effective method of defence. When it feels threatened, the spitting cobra rises up in typical cobra fashion, extending its hood, which is quite narrow by cobra standards. Holding its head high off the ground, it then spits large quantities of venom over a distance of more than 2m (6.5ft), aiming for the attacker's eyes.

The venom is very potent, causing blindness if it does reach the eyes, and bites can be fatal to humans. These cobras, however, are very reluctant to bite, preferring a "spit-and-run" tactic, making off while their enemy's eyes are stinging. Of course, cobras do not hold back when they come across prey animals. These are rapidly killed by the powerful venom injected via the snake's fangs.

Adults are predominantly nocturnal, hiding inside termite hills, old logs or piles of leaves during the day. Young cobras are more active during the day, and with good cause: bumping into an adult can have disastrous consequences as spitting cobras are occasionally cannibalistic.

The colour of spitting cobras is very variable. Individuals may be red, yellow, pinkish or steely grey. Cobras (Naja genus) are a sizeable group associated more with Asia.

Black mamba

Dendroaspis polylepis

The black mamba is probably Africa's most feared snake, and justifiably so. It is an aggressive animal, armed with venom capable of killing humans in less than four hours. However, its reputation for unprovoked attacks on humans is unjustified. A black mamba will only attack if it feels threatened. Nonetheless, when it does attack it rarely fails to bite.

Raising its head up off the ground to a height of 1.2m (4ft), black mouth agape, the mamba charges. It can reach a speed of 16kph (10mph), making it one of the fastest snakes in the world.

Clearly the black mamba is a very successful predator. Hunting by day using its excellent eyesight, it usually bites its prey a couple of times and then lets go. The stricken animal may make off but in a very short time it is paralyzed by the snake's toxins, and then swallowed headfirst. Mambas often attack birds, shooting into the air as the birds try to fly away. Adult black mambas are so formidable that they have no natural predators.

Distribution: Southern and central Africa.
Habitat: Tropical forests and savannah.
Food: Mainly small mammals and birds.
Size: 3.5m (11.5ft).
Maturity: Not known.
Breeding: Clutches of 14 eggs laid after a long courtship period.
Life span: 26 years.
Status: Common.

Black mambas are actually grey with white bellies. Their name refers to the colour of the insides of their mouths.

Royal python

Python regius

Royal pythons are Africa's smallest pythons. They are generally active at night, when they hunt using eyes that are well adapted to low light levels. They also have special heat-sensing pits around their mouths to detect prey in the dark. Since these pits pick up heat in the form of infrared radiation, they are well equipped to detect the body heat released by their prey.

Pythons are not venomous; they are constrictors. They grab hold of their prey and throw a number of coils around it, holding so tightly that the animal cannot breathe. Constrictors do not crush their prey; they suffocate them.

During the hot dry season, pythons lie inactive (aestivate) in underground burrows. They emerge when the rains arrive in order to mate. However, royal pythons only mate once every three or four years, so that they reproduce at a low rate. This means that their populations are particularly vulnerable to over-hunting. Royal pythons are endangered in the wild because they are collected for the pet trade, as well as being hunted for their flesh and skins.

Distribution: Central Africa.
Habitat: Grassland.
Food: Small mammals, birds, lizards and other species of snakes.
Size: 1.2m (4ft).
Maturity: 3–5 years.
Breeding: 4–10 unusually large eggs.
Life span: 25 years.
Status: Threatened

Royal pythons are also known as ball pythons because when they are threatened they coil up into tight balls with their heads well protected inside.

Forest cobra (*Naja melanoleuca*): 1.5–3m (5–10ft)
The forest cobra holds the record, along with the anaconda, for being the longest-living snake. It is capable of reaching the ripe old age of 30 years. It is found all over western and southern Africa, inhabiting many different habitats. Forest cobras have a reputation for being ill-tempered and dangerous. Their venom is highly toxic. They chase attackers off with mouths agape and ready to bite.

African house snake (*Lamprophis fuliginosus*): 0.6–1.2m (2–4ft); 200–500g (0.4–1.1lb)
One of the most successful of all the snakes in Africa, the African house snake is found virtually everywhere south and west of the Sahara Desert. It is a species that has learned to live alongside people, who tolerate it because it feeds on rodents.

Rinkhal (*Hemachatus haemachatus*): 1–1.5m (3.25–5ft)
Rinkhals closely resemble cobras in that they have "hoods" that they spread when feeling threatened. Found in southern Africa, they differ from true cobras by having differently shaped scales, and by giving birth to live young (whereas cobras lay eggs). In the wild rinkhals mainly eat toads, but will make meals of any small animals unfortunate enough to come too close.

Malagasy leaf-nosed snake

Langaha madagascariensis

Also known as twig mimic snakes, the habits of these peculiar-looking snakes are not very well known. Lying motionless for hours in the canopy of the tropical forests of Madagascar, leaf-nosed snakes blend into their background incredibly well, becoming extremely difficult to spot. Their camouflage is perfected by the remarkable protrusions from the front of their faces. Males possess long, spiky projections, making them look even more like twigs, whereas the females have leaf-like structures instead.

Leaf-nosed snakes are only active for about one hour in every day, normally waiting until midday, the hottest part of the day, before rousing themselves to go hunting. By remaining inactive, the snakes save a lot of energy, which allows them to have long breaks between foraging trips. A decent meal can keep a leaf-nosed snake going for four days or more, before it feels the need to go hunting again.

Distribution: Madagascar.
Habitat: Tropical rainforests and dry forests.
Food: Tree frogs, small birds and reptiles.
Size: 1m (3.25ft); 50–80g (0.1–0.2lb).
Maturity: Not known.
Breeding: Clutches of around 10 eggs laid in November or December.
Life span: 10 years.
Status: Common.

The leaf-like snout of the Malagasy leaf-nosed snake helps to camouflage it among leaves and twigs.

CATS

Of all the carnivores, the cats have the highest proportion of meat in their diets. Typically, cats hunt alone by night, using their acute senses of hearing, sight and scent to locate and stalk their prey. Once within pouncing distance, they unsheath their curved claws, which are used to grip the prey as the cat delivers fatal neck bites with dagger-shaped teeth.

Lion

Panthera leo

Male lions have thick manes of hair, while the females do not. The manes are symbols of the dominance level in males.

The social behaviour of lions is unique among wild cats. A typical pride contains about ten related females with their cubs and one or two males. Females do most of the hunting. They may work together to isolate and kill large prey such as zebra or buffalo. Males in a pride help themselves to the females' kills and rarely hunt for themselves. They spend much of the night patrolling, marking territory and driving away rival males. A pride male's reign rarely lasts longer than three years before he is usurped. Once adolescent males are evicted from the prides where they were born and reared, they may stay together in hunting groups, or hunt alone before eventually joining other groups.

Distribution: Africa, south of the Sahara, and Gir Forest, India.
Habitat: Open country.
Food: Grazing animals.
Size: 2–2.7m (6.5–9ft); 125–180kg (275–396lb).
Maturity: 3–4 years.
Breeding: 1 litter of 2–5 cubs in alternate years.
Life span: 16 years.
Status: Vulnerable.

Cheetah

Acinonyx jubatus

Distribution: Most of Africa, Middle East to Turkestan.
Habitat: Savannah and open, dry grassland.
Food: Gazelles or antelopes.
Size: 1.6–2.1m (5.25–7ft); 30–45kg (66–99lb).
Maturity: Females 3 years; males 3–4 years.
Breeding: 2–6 kittens every 2–3 years.
Life span: 15–20 years.
Status: Endangered.

Cheetahs differ from typical cats in several ways. Instead of stealth, they use speed to run down their prey, assisted by blunt claws that grip the ground. The dew-claws, however, which are used to grasp the prey, are curved and sharp. A cheetah is built like a racing dog, with a small head and long legs and body, but the teeth and jaws are too small and weak to deliver an effective death bite, so the cheetah is forced to suffocate its prey. After the sustained effort of catching and killing a prey animal, a cheetah may need to rest for half an hour before starting to eat.

The cheetah is well known as the fastest animal on land. Sadly, despite captive breeding programmes, it is now an endangered species. A breeding female requires a hunting range of up to 800sq km (300sq miles) and, apart from some national parks and isolated populations, suitable territories are mainly restricted to Namibia and parts of South Africa.

The cheetah's long, flexible spine helps to lengthen the stride of the animal at full sprint. It is the fastest terrestrial animal, capable of sprinting at 110kph (70mph).

Eurasian lynx

Lynx lynx

Eurasian lynx have three distinct coat patterns: stripes, spots or plain. These markings can be either faint or clearly visible.

This golden, delicately marked cat hunts small game by night in cool mountain forests and woodland. A shortened tail helps to conserve body heat, but it hinders communication between cats to a certain degree. As with other short-tailed cats that live in cold climates, the lynx has developed conspicuous ear-tufts to send visual signals instead.

Lack of a tail also impairs a cat's balance when running and climbing; the lynx hunts mainly by the techniques of stealth or ambush. Its feet are densely furred, even on the pads, giving a good grip as well as warmth on frozen ground. Most lynxes live in dense forests, but they may also wander into more open country. They build rough beds under rocks and fallen trees, or inside shrubs, resting during the day and hunting at night. While out and about, the lynx climbs trees and fords rivers – swimming if necessary – as it travels far and wide in search of food. It relies on its senses of vision and smell to locate prey, which it then stalks through the trees.

Distribution: Eastern Europe, Pyrenees and northern Eurasia, with distinct races in some regions.
Habitat: Montane forest and woodland.
Food: Rabbits, hares, birds and small deer.
Size: 0.8–1.3m (2.5–4.25ft); 18–21kg (40–46lb).
Maturity: 12–15 months.
Breeding: 2–4 cubs, weaned at 12 weeks, independent at 12 months.
Life span: 10–20 years.
Status: Endangered in south-eastern Europe.

European wildcat (*Felis sylvestris sylvestris*): 36–76cm (14–30in); up to 5kg (11lb)
In parts of its forest range, extending from Scotland to eastern Europe, this subspecies interbreeds with domestic cats, making its pedigree uncertain. The pure wildcat resembles a large, robust dark grey tabby cat, with short legs and a bushy, blunt-tipped tail. Unlike feral domestic cats, it is entirely solitary apart from a brief association between males and females in the mating season.

African wildcat (*Felis sylvestris lybica*): 30–75cm (12–30in); up to 5kg (11lb)
Whereas the European wildcat avoids people, its sandy-coloured, lightly-striped African counterpart frequently lives around human settlements. The ancient Egyptians, who are credited with domesticating the cat, would have been familiar with this subspecies. These are two reasons for believing it to be the chief ancestor of domestic cats. Genetic fingerprinting also points strongly towards the African wildcat as our modern pet's ancestor.

Caracal

Caracal caracal

The name caracal is Turkish for "black ears". Caracals are also known as desert lynxes because they have short tails and ear-tufts like their northern cousins, an adaptation for cold weather. This has led scientists to conclude that the caracal's ancestors once lived in colder regions.

This adaptation to the cold comes in handy during the night, when caracals generally hunt. It is not unusual for desert temperatures to plunge below 0°C (32°F). Caracals prey on anything they can find and kill, including insects, snakes, lizards, gazelles and even brooding ostriches.

Caracals set up home in the abandoned burrows of porcupines or any other suitable crevices. Like other types of lynx, the caracal hunts at night, stealing up close to its prey before leaping the last few metres in huge bounds. The caracal is the fastest cat of its size. Prey is stalked and then captured after a quick dash or leap. The caracal is easy to tame and has been used as a hunting cat in Iran and India. However, it is also persecuted in this region as a pest.

Distribution: Southern Africa to Senegal and India, excluding the Congo and Arabian Desert.
Habitat: Dry scrubland, but avoids sand areas.
Food: Rodents, hyraxes, hares and small antelopes.
Size: 66–76cm (26–30in); 18kg (40lb).
Maturity: 6 months to 2 years.
Breeding: Litter of 3 young born every year.
Life span: 15 years.
Status: Lower risk (threatened in Asia).

Caracals have narrow, pointed ears with long tufts of hair at their tips. These are used to signal to other cats.

HYENAS

Hyenas are heavily built, long-legged and long-necked carnivores with large, padded feet and short, hairy tails. Their front legs are longer than their back legs and their shaggy coats are either striped or spotted. There are four species, all of which live in Africa. The striped hyena, the widest-ranging species, also lives in Turkey, the Middle East and parts of India.

Spotted hyena

Crocuta crocuta

Spotted hyenas are dog-like, with sloping backs and long thick necks. They are the only mammal to disgorge indigestible hair, along with hooves, pieces of horn and bone, and grass.

Spotted hyenas live in female-dominated groups known as clans. The mothers rear all of the cubs together in a communal breeding den that is only big enough for the cubs to enter. The entrance to the den is guarded by one or two adults, helping to reduce the number of young killed by other carnivores or hyenas.

Spotted hyenas have a complicated greeting ceremony, involving a variety of interactions using scents and physical gestures. These are only used by certain individuals in a clan and are uncommon between females and low-ranking males. They help to reduce stress in the group. Females are very aggressive and, to help them dominate their clans, they have developed false genitals to look like males. They will fight other females to win over and mate with favoured males. Hyenas are very vocal and their wails – howling screams and "laughter" – can inform other clan members of a food source from up to 5km (3 miles) away.

Distribution: Most of Africa outside rainforest.
Habitat: Woodlands, savannahs, subdeserts, forest edges and mountains.
Food: Hunt antelope, buffalo and zebra. Scavenge from the kills of other large carnivores.
Size: 1.2–1.8m (4–5.75ft); 60–80kg (132–176lb).
Maturity: Cubs weaned after 18 months.
Breeding: Litter of 1–2 cubs born at any time of the year.
Life span: 12 years, and up to 25 years in captivity.
Status: Declining in all areas.

Aardwolf

Proteles cristatus

The aardwolf is a specialist feeder and mainly consumes harvester termites. These give off a very toxic spray, and few other predators are able to overcome the chemicals emitted. Aardwolfs find the termites by listening for their movements.

Unlike the spotted hyenas which have large crushing teeth, aardwolfs only have small peg-like teeth, ideal for crunching small insects. The aardwolf is mainly nocturnal and lives alone, in pairs or in small family groups. Females often live together in the same den to help increase the chances of survival for their pups. Burrows are either taken over from other species or dug by the aardwolfs themselves.

When feeding, adults may travel up to 10km (6 miles) in one night and in this time they may consume 250,000 termites. When threatened, they raise their long manes and erect their tails but, unusually, they keep their mouths closed – the aardwolf has such tiny teeth that it would appear almost harmless if it opened its mouth.

The aardwolf is slimmer and more agile than the other three species of hyena. When attacked, the aardwolf raises the mane along its back and secretes a foul-smelling odour from its anal glands.

Distribution: Southern Africa and north-east Africa.
Habitat: Heavily grazed and trampled grasslands, and sandy plains and plateaux.
Food: Termites plus other invertebrates including grasshoppers and maggots.
Size: 0.8–1m (2.5–3.25ft); 6–11kg (13–24lb).
Maturity: Weaned after 16 weeks.
Breeding: Litter of 1–4 pups born at any time of the year.
Life span: Not known.
Status: Uncommon.

DOGS

There are several members of the wild dog family, Canidae, *including the African hunting dog, Ethiopian wolf, foxes and jackals. Long legs and muzzles enable these mammals to chase and capture prey. Most have a bushy tail and feet with four toes at the back and five at the front. Small canids are solitary hunters, medium-sized canids hunt alone or in small family groups and large canids hunt in large cooperative groups.*

African hunting dog

Lycaon pictus

Hunting dogs are highly social and live in large packs of around 100 animals. A pack is formed by a group of brothers from one pack meeting with a group of sisters from another. A dominant pair emerges and breeds. Females will fight each other for the top breeding position.

These dogs are truly nomadic carnivores. They are on the move all the time to mark their territories and to avoid conflict with lions. Movement is reduced when there are small pups in the den. Unlike most canids which howl to show their presence, wild dogs use scents that last for months. When packs contain about 20 adults, the older offspring leave to form subgroups and hunt independently.

Individual dogs are capable of killing large prey such as impala antelope, although most hunting is done in packs. Pups typically leave at two to three years of age but sometimes stay to help rear more young. Packs stay together for no more than six years, usually two, when the founder members die. The remaining dogs separate into single-sex groups to find new opposite-sex groups and start all over again.

The African hunting dog has black, white, brown and yellow-brown blotches. It has large, round ears, a broad, black muzzle and a tufted tail, usually with a white tip. It is also the only carnivore except hyenas to have five toes on all four feet.

Distribution: Non-forested, non-desert areas of Africa.
Habitat: Desert plains, open and wooded savannah, and bushed country.
Food: Antelope, eland, buffalo and wildebeest.
Size: 1–1.5m (3.25–5ft); 17–36kg (37–79lb).
Maturity: Pups follow pack after 3 months and join in hunting at 12–14 months.
Breeding: Average of 7–10 pups born in the dry winter months from March–July in the south.
Life span: Not known.
Status: Endangered.

Ethiopian wolf

Canis simensis

Ethiopian wolves' main prey are giant mole rats (*Tachyoryctes macrocephalus*), which make up nearly half of their diet when available. During the day, the wolves lie on the mounds made by the giant mole rats. These make good ambush sites to catch their prey. Ethiopian wolves live in packs with two or more adult females, five closely related males and the current offspring of the dominant pair. The females do not always mate with the males in their pack; indeed three-quarters of matings may be with males from neighbouring packs.

These wolves are extremely vocal, using all types of howls, yelps and screams to mark their territories, which may be 2.4–12sq km (1–4.5sq miles) in size. They forage alone, but the animals will meet in the morning, midday and evening to rest, play, sleep, feed their pups and mark boundaries. This is when they are most vocal.

Ethiopian wolves have reddish-ginger coats, with white throat patches, inner ears, underparts and lower legs, and dark tails. They have long legs, long muzzles and squared-off noses and upper lips.

Distribution: Restricted to the Ethiopian Highlands of Africa.
Habitat: Alpine moorlands.
Food: Naked mole rats and other rodents, hares and antelope calves.
Size: 1.3m (4.25ft); 11–19kg (24–42lb).
Maturity: Not known.
Breeding: 2–6 pups born from August–December.
Life span: Not known.
Status: Critically endangered.

Black-backed jackal

Canis mesomelas

Distribution: Southern Africa and East Africa.
Habitat: Dry savannahs.
Food: Omnivorous diet.
Size: 0.7–1.3m (2.25–4.25ft); 6–12kg (13–26lb).
Maturity: Not known.
Breeding: Usually 3–4 pups born July–October in southern Africa.
Life span: Not known.
Status: Not endangered.

The black-backed jackal is reddish-brown with a white-streaked black band along its back. The thick, hairy tail is also black, particularly at the tip. In parts of South Africa, black-backed jackals used to cause problems by feeding on large numbers of pineapples.

Black-backed jackals live in closely bonded pairs, sometimes with one or two older offspring staying to help rear the pups. The older offspring increase the survival rate of young pups by providing extra food and guarding the den from predators, such as hyenas. When the parents arrive back from hunting, the pups start begging and this encourages the adults to regurgitate food which they have caught and swallowed earlier.

The jackals communicate with screaming yells followed by three or four short yaps. They make these calls more often during the winter when they start mating. In South Africa, where black-backed jackals are the only species of jackal present, howling is common.

Black-backed jackals have very varied diets, feeding on anything from young antelope, rodents and hares through to birds, reptiles, carrion, invertebrates, wild berries and fruit.

Red fox

Vulpes vulpes

The red fox is a very successful and adaptable species. It is mainly active at night but will forage during the day, particularly when there are hungry cubs to feed. It also enjoys curling up and sunbathing in exposed but private spots, often by railway lines or roadsides.

A pair of foxes shares a home range, often with young from the previous breeding season. Mating takes place from December to February and after a few months, females – also known as vixens – give birth to between 3 and 12 cubs. The availability of food determines whether vixens breed and how many cubs they produce. During the mating season, females and occasionally males give out spine-tingling shrieks.

Red foxes mark their territories with a distinctive scent, which lingers and tells when a fox has been in the area. The scent is left with urine or faeces and is produced by special glands at the base of the tail. There are further scent glands between the pads of foxes' feet and around their lips.

The red fox is a large fox with a rusty, red-brown coat and a darker bushy tail with a white tip.

Distribution: Europe, Asia and North Africa. Introduced to Australia.
Habitat: Able to colonize almost any habitat available.
Food: Small vertebrates, invertebrates, kitchen scraps, fruit and carrion.
Size: 85–95cm (34–38in); 4–8kg (9–18lb).
Maturity: 10 months.
Breeding: 3–12 pups born in early spring.
Life span: 9 years.
Status: Common.

Fennec fox

Vulpes zerda

The fennec fox is the world's smallest fox and lives in the hot deserts of North Africa. The animal gets most of its water from solid food. Its body also ensures that the least amount of water is wasted. Fennec foxes are only active at night, when the temperature is much lower.

The fox's very large ears are used to detect the sounds made by prey, such as grasshoppers and other insects, in or on the sand. The large ears also radiate excess body heat. Cream-coloured fur helps keep fennec foxes well camouflaged against the sand when resting during the day. They are able to dig very quickly to catch any fast-moving prey living in the sand.

Fennec foxes are usually seen in pairs. In the breeding season, females are very protective of their pups and will be very aggressive if anything threatens them.

The fennec fox is a small cream-coloured fox with short legs, huge ears, a small pointed muzzle and a black-tipped tail.

Distribution: Sahara Desert through to the Nubian Desert. Also found in North Arabia.
Habitat: Sandy deserts.
Food: Various animal and plant foods, particularly insects.
Size: 42–72cm (17–29in); 1–1.5kg (2.2–3.3lb).
Maturity: Suckled for 2 months and mature by 6 months of age.
Breeding: Mating between January and February. Give birth to 1–5 pups.
Life span: Not known
Status: Common.

Sand or **pale fox** (*Vulpes pallida*): 61–74cm (24–30in); 2–3.6kg (4.4–8lb)
Found across the Sahel belt in northern Africa, the sand fox lives in family parties comprising an adult pair and their offspring. They dig their own burrows to a depth of 2–3m (6.5–10ft) and then extend them for a farther 15m (50ft). They come out at night or early evening to feed on fruit and berries, which provide them with their daily supplement of water. The sand fox feeds on small mammals and insects.

Royal or **hoary fox** (*Vulpes cana*): 40–60cm (16–24in); 2–3kg (4.4–6.6lb)
A shy cat-like fox with very dense, sandy-coloured fur, the royal fox can be found from Pakistan to northern Egypt, living in rock crevices and shelters. It has excellent hearing to find and eat insects. It will also feed on berries. The tail is long with thick fur, which is thought to help the animal evade predators that may try to catch it. If a predator grasps the tail, the royal fox has a chance to run away even if it means the predator being left with a mouthful of fur or even a piece of the tail itself.

Cape fox (*Vulpes chama*): 86–97cm (34–39in); 2.4–4kg (5.25–8.8lb)
The Cape fox is found nowhere else in the world apart from southern Africa – the Cape. It is a small, slim fox with large pointed ears, and lives in open areas where it can feed on a wide range of food, from small rodents and insects to reptiles and birds. Cape foxes live in burrow dens dug out by other mammals, usually hidden among thick vegetation and rocks.

Bat-eared fox

Otocyon megalotis

Bat-eared foxes have very large ears that listen for the movements of harvester termites. Their very thick fur coats protect the foxes from the painful bites of soldier termites that they encounter. They have 46–50 teeth, whereas most mammals have far fewer than this. Their teeth are used to slice up insects that have hard shells and pincers. With the ability to move their lower jaws up and down five times a second, insects are hurriedly chewed and eaten. The bat-eared fox also has very strong claws on its front feet, enabling it to dig very fast.

A pair normally lives together with up to six offspring. They mate for life and have a home range that may be 0.25–3sq km (0.1–1sq miles) in size. Sometimes a second female will join the pair and share the breeding den. Individuals feed by walking long distances over their territories, continually listening for small invertebrates. When they hear something underground, they dig vigorously, catching the prey before it has a chance to get away.

Bat-eared foxes are smaller than most canids. They have huge ears and dark, bushy tails.

Distribution: Southern Africa and East Africa.
Habitat: Open country, including short scrub, grassland, steppes, lightly wooded areas and farmland.
Food: Harvester termites, beetles and other insects.
Size: 75–90cm (30–36in); 3–5kg (6.6–11lb).
Maturity: Not known.
Breeding: 1–6 pups born from September–November.
Life span: Not known.
Status: Common.

SMALL CARNIVORES

Some of the small carnivores, the mustelids, are very fast and efficient hunters. They can tackle prey much larger than themselves. Mustelids tend to be solitary animals, defending their territories from all comers. Their long, lithe bodies, short legs and sharp claws mean that they are often skilful climbers, capable of reaching the most inaccessible of places and leaving their prey few places to hide.

Stoat

Mustela erminea

Although rarely seen, stoats are common in the countryside, where they mainly feed on rodents. However, the large males will often prey on rabbits, even though rabbits are considerably larger. Stoats are famed for mesmerizing their prey by dancing around them, before nipping in for the kill. This is not just an old wives' tale. Stoats have been observed leaping around near rabbits in a seemingly deranged fashion. This curious "dance" seems to have the effect of confusing the rabbits, which just watch the stoat draw slowly closer and closer, until it is too late to escape.

As winter approaches, populations of stoats that live in cooler, northern areas change the colour of their coats. In summer, they are a chestnut colour but, by the time the first snows have fallen, the stoats have changed to pure white. White stoats are known as ermines, and their fur was once prized for its pure colour and soft feel.

In mild climates, stoats have chestnut fur all year round. In colder areas, they moult into white fur in winter. Stoats are distinguished from their smaller cousins, the weasels, by having black tips to their tails.

Distribution: Widespread in northern and central Europe extending into Asia and across northern North America. Introduced to New Zealand.
Habitat: Anywhere with enough cover.
Food: Mammals up to the size of rabbits.
Size: 16–31cm (6.5–12.5in); 140–445g (0.3–1lb).
Maturity: 1 year.
Breeding: 1 litter per year of 5–12 young.
Life span: 10 years.
Status: Common.

Zorilla

Ictonyx striatus

Zorillas have an uncanny resemblance to skunks, although they are more closely related to ferrets and polecats. Their alternative name is the striped polecat. Not only do they share black and white markings with their North American relatives, but they also eject a foul-smelling liquid from glands near their anuses if alarmed. When faced with enemies, zorillas puff up their fur in an attempt to look bigger, and then squirt their noxious liquid towards their assailants. If the liquid gets in a predator's eyes, it causes intense irritation, as well as smelling very unpleasant. This strategy is extremely effective, with few predators prepared to risk the stinking spray.

Zorillas are nocturnal animals, resting during the day in burrows or rock crevices. At night they hunt small animals, as well as eating the eggs of ground-nesting birds, which are a particular favourite. Zorillas are predominantly ground-living animals, but they are proficient swimmers and climbers when the need arises.

With their bold black and white markings, zorillas are easily mistaken for skunks.

Distribution: Sudan to South Africa.
Habitat: A wide variety, including temperate forest, tropical forest, savannah and grasslands.
Food: Rodents, large insects, eggs, snakes, birds, frogs and reptiles.
Size: 33–38cm (13–15in); 1kg (2.2lb).
Maturity: 1 year.
Breeding: 1 litter of 1–3 young born each year.
Life span: 13 years.
Status: Common.

Badger

Meles meles

Large members of the mustelid family, badgers have a much more diverse diet than most of the small carnivores. Adept at making a meal out of most situations, badgers will eat anything they find, including berries, fungi and carrion. Worms are a particularly favourite, and on warm, damp nights badgers can regularly be observed patrolling through pastureland, searching them out.

One of the badger's greatest assets is its mouth. The way a badger's skull is structured means that it is physically impossible for the animal to dislocate its jaw, allowing badgers to have one of the most powerful bites in the natural world. This trait makes the badger a fearsome foe for any animal that happens to cross its path.

Unlike most other mustelids, badgers are very social animals. They live in large family groups centred on communal dens, or setts.

The badger's black and white face makes it instantly recognizable.

Distribution: Throughout Europe (but not north of Arctic circle) and Asia.
Habitat: Favours a mixture of woodland and pastureland, also moving into urban habitats.
Food: Omnivorous diet.
Size: 65–80cm (26–32in); 8–12kg (17.5–26.5lb).
Maturity: 1–2 years.
Breeding: 1 litter of 1–5 young per year.
Life span: 15 years.
Status: Common.

Sable (*Martes zibellina*): 32–46cm (12–18.5in), 0.9–1.8kg (2–4lb)
Restricted to the northern forests of Siberia, the sable has a long, thick, soft coat which protects it from the cold. Largely solitary, the sable may occupy home ranges of up to 25sq km (8sq miles) of forestland. It needs this amount of land to provide it with enough food in the harsh conditions of its habitat.

Weasel (*Mustela nivalis*): 17–30cm (6.8–12in); 30–70g (0.06–0.15lb)
Similar, but much smaller than their close relatives the stoats, weasels are fierce mini-predators. The weasel's tail lacks the black tip of the stoat's. In Scandinavia these brown mustelids turn white in winter. Females may live up to three years, giving birth to litters of around five kittens in their second and third years. Males have even more fast and furious lives. The onus is on travelling far and wide, looking for mates. This makes them much more vulnerable to predation, and male weasels rarely live long enough to see their first birthday.

Beech marten

Martes foina

Not found in Britain but common in continental Europe, the beech marten was originally an animal of woodland and hilly habitats. However, it has greatly increased its range by exploiting the habitats humans have created. In some regions of France, Germany and Switzerland, beech martens have become very common in towns, frequently occupying the loft spaces of people's homes.

They can actually be quite a nuisance, chewing electrical wiring and making off with roof insulation to use as bedding. Beech martens have also been reported to have developed a liking for cars. The learned behaviour of sleeping under car bonnets, where it's nice and warm, has spread across central Europe. Every day, up to 40 cars in Switzerland are damaged by beech martens chewing through the wires under their bonnets. This compulsive chewing behaviour is a consequence of the marten's dietary flexibility. Youngsters will test anything and everything to see if it is edible or not.

Beech martens have a silky dark-brown coat with a white throat patch. People tolerate them in towns partly because they help to control rodents. Their main enemies are birds of prey and foxes.

Distribution: Throughout Europe.
Habitat: Deciduous woodland, open rocky hillsides and urban habitats.
Food: Rodents, fruit and eggs.
Size: 42–48cm (16–19in); 1.3–2.3kg (2.8–5lb).
Maturity: 1–2 years.
Breeding: 1 litter of 1–8 kittens per year.
Life span: 18 years.
Status: Common.

MONGOOSES AND CAT-LIKE ANIMALS

Mongooses, civets and genets form a group of small carnivores called the viverrids. In general, viverrids have long, slender bodies with short legs and sharp snouts. They can be split into two broad groups. Mongooses have weasel-like bodies and tend to live in large units, or bands, in open country, while genets and civets look more like cats, and mostly live solitary lives in dense forest.

Banded mongoose

Mungos mungo

Distribution: Africa south of the Sahara.
Habitat: Grassland and dry woodland.
Food: Insects and millipedes.
Size: 30–45cm (12–18in); 1.5–2.5kg (3.3–5.5lb).
Maturity: 9–10 months.
Breeding: Litters of 3 or 4, up to 4 times per year.
Life span: Up to 12 years.
Status: Common.

The banded mongoose is one of the most common mongooses in Africa. It lives in open grassland and areas of dry woodland, and is also found in rocky, broken country. It lives in bands of up to 40 individuals, sharing dens inside old termite mounds or abandoned aardvark holes. The dens have central sleeping chambers, which are reached from several holes.

Dens are used for only a few days at a time, with bands regularly moving on to new foraging sites. Banded mongooses feed during the daytime, returning to their dens before sunset. Their diet consists of invertebrates, such as beetles and millipedes.

Banded mongooses have excellent senses of smell, hearing and vision. Their bands are highly social, with members rarely straying far from each other and communicating by making several distinct sounds. All females in a band breed at the same time. The young are raised together, and are suckled by all the adult females in the band.

Banded mongooses have brownish-grey fur with dark brown stripes, or bands, across their backs and tails. Each foot possesses five long claws.

Meerkat

Suricata suricatta

Meerkats are relatives of mongooses, which live in large bands in the arid, semi-desert areas of southern Africa. They are efficient diggers and live in large underground burrows.

Meerkats live in highly organized societies. While feeding, at least one band member keeps a look-out for danger, communicating to the others with an array of sounds. For example, howling warns that a bird of prey is approaching, while double-barking informs the band that a terrestrial predator, has been spotted.

A meerkat band has between 10 and 15 individuals, with two or three pairs of males and females which do all the breeding. The young kits stay close to their dens and are looked after by at least one adult while the rest of their band forages for food.

Meerkats live in dry, open country in southern Africa, especially in the semi-desert regions of Namibia, southern Angola, Botswana and western South Africa.

Distribution: South-western and southern Africa from Angola to South Africa.
Habitat: Semi-desert and scrubland.
Food: Insects, scorpions, small vertebrates and eggs.
Size: 25–35cm (10–14in); 600–975g (1.3–2.1lb).
Maturity: 1 year.
Breeding: Litters of 2–5 kits born once per year in November.
Life span: 10 years.
Status: Common.

Common genet

Genetta genetta

A row of black erectile hairs is usually present along the middle of the back of the common genet. The tail has black and white rings. A genet's claws can be withdrawn inside the paws, just like a cat's.

Common genets, also called small-spotted genets, are related to civets. They are common in Africa, and a few are found in western Europe, although biologists think that these are descended from genets introduced to the area many years ago.

Genets live alone or in pairs, resting by day in sheltered spots or abandoned burrows. They feed at night, hunting for small animals in a range of habitats, from dense forest to open grassland. They climb trees to prey on roosting birds or silently stalk victims on the ground.

Genets mainly communicate by sound and smell, but also use their tails to signal. In warmer parts, genets breed during the wet season, with a few females managing to produce two litters each year.

Distribution: South-western Europe, including France and Spain, and Africa, excluding tropical rainforests and deserts.
Habitat: Forests and grasslands.
Food: Rodents, birds, small reptiles and insects.
Size: Length 42–58cm (16–23in); 1–3kg (2.2–6.6lb).
Maturity: 4 years.
Breeding: 2 litters of 1–4 kittens every year.
Life span: 13 years.
Status: Common.

Aquatic genet (*Osbornictis piscivora*): 45cm (17in); 1.5g (3.3lb)
These are very rare cat-like animals found in the dense tropical forests of the Congo. Their fur is chestnut-red, their tails are black and they have white spots between their eyes. This species is thought to live alone and spend a lot of time in or near water, feeding on fish and frogs. Unlike other genets, aquatic genets do not have hairs on their palms, which may help them feel for prey in muddy water holes.

Cusimanse (*Crossarchus obscurus*): 30–45cm (12–18in); 1.5kg (3.3lb)
Cusimanses are small mongooses that live in patches of swampy forest in West Africa. Their bodies are covered in long brown-grey-yellow hairs. Cusimanses travel in groups and appear to be active both day and night, taking shelter when convenient. They feed on fruit, seeds, insects and small reptiles. Cusimanses also crack open snail shells and eggs by hurling them between their back legs on to hard stones.

African civet (*Civettictis civetta*): 68–89cm (27–35in); 7–20kg (15–44lb)
The African civet lives all over sub-Saharan Africa, being equally at home in open grassland and dense forest. Its coarse hair is black with yellowish spots and stripes. During the day, civets hide in thickets of grass. At night they cross large distances, even swimming across rivers, in search of carrion, small animals, eggs, insects and fruit. African civets live alone and only settle in one place when nursing young. Breeding takes place throughout the year.

Fossa

Cryptoprocta ferox

The fossa is the largest carnivore in Madagascar. Looking very similar to a cat, it hunts by leaping through the trees to prey on lemurs and other small animals, such as birds and frogs. The fossa lives alone, patrolling its forest territory at dawn and dusk and sheltering in caves or inside disused termite mounds by day.

Fossas sometimes attack domestic animals, such as pigs and poultry, and are often killed as pests by people, who also unnecessarily fear that the fossas may attack them. This persecution, combined with the destruction of their forest habitat, means that fossas have become very rare, like much of Madagascar's native wildlife.

Fossas only spend time with other members of their species during the breeding season, which is in September and October. The females give birth three months later, in the height of summer.

Fossas walk in a flat-footed manner on their soles, like bears, rather than on their toes, like cats.

Distribution: Madagascar.
Habitat: Forests.
Food: Rodents, birds, frogs, reptiles and young lemurs.
Size: 61–80cm (24–32in); 7–12kg (15–26.5lb).
Maturity: 4 years.
Breeding: Twins born once per year.
Life span: 17 years
Status: Endangered.

RODENTS

The Rodentia, *with over 2,000 species distributed all around the globe, is by far the largest order of mammals. All rodents have two upper and two lower chisel-like incisor teeth. These incisors grow continuously throughout their lives, so they can gnaw anything and everything without the possibility of their teeth getting worn down.*

Edible dormouse

Glis glis

When awake, all species of dormouse belie their dozy reputation, being incredibly lithe and agile climbers – the edible dormouse being no exception. These dormice spend virtually their entire lives in the treetops, searching for food, and are very reluctant to leave the safety of the branches. If they cannot leap between trees, they will not cross the open areas on the ground. Roads and tracks cut through woodland can therefore inhibit the movement of dormice.

Dormice are champion sleepers, being one of the few types of mammal to enter a true state of hibernation. Come autumn, dormice descend into the bases of hollow trees, wrap themselves into balls and fall into a state of very deep sleep. They allow their body temperature to drop very low, barely more than the temperature of the air around them. Heart rate and breathing also slow right down. By doing this, they are able to conserve enough energy to last them through the winter. When spring arrives, the dormice's metabolism speeds up again, bringing them out of six or seven months of uninterrupted sleep.

Also known as fat dormice, the Romans kept edible dormice in jars, called gliraria, to fatten them for the table.

Distribution: Throughout central and eastern Europe, extending west through northern Spain. Introduced into England.
Habitat: The canopy of mature deciduous woodland.
Food: Nuts, fruit, fungi, bark, insects and occasionally eggs and nestlings.
Size: 13–19cm (5–7.5in), 70–300g (0.15–0.66lb).
Maturity: 2 years.
Breeding: 1 litter of 2–9 offspring born in summer.
Life span: 7 years.
Status: Common.

Water vole

Arvicola terrestris

Distribution: Widespread across Europe and Asia.
Habitat: Banks of slow-flowing rivers and streams.
Food: Grasses, rushes and sedges.
Size: 14–22cm (5.5–8.8in); 150–300g (0.33–0.66lb).
Maturity: 2 months.
Breeding: 3 or 4 litters of 5 young born throughout spring and summer.
Life span: Up to 3 years.
Status: Common.

Water voles are also known – confusingly – as water rats. Ratty, of *The Wind in the Willows* fame, was really a water vole, and like him, these rodents are found living alongside slow-moving rivers, ditches, dykes and lakes. In areas of central Europe, however, water voles do not live by water, preferring dry habitats instead. In some places they are considered to be a serious agricultural pest.

Water voles excavate extensive burrow systems in the banks of the rivers, with plenty of entrance and exit holes so that they can escape from the various predators they encounter – both in and out of the water. Even so, the average life span of a water vole is a mere five months. Herons, barn owls, brown rats and pike are all known to prey on water voles, but the rodents' most important predators are stoats and mink. Indeed, the introduction of the American mink to Britain has been blamed for the species' recent and rapid decline.

Water voles are often mistaken for rats, but they differ from rats by having blunter snouts, more rounded bodies, smaller ears and shorter, hairy tails.

Siberian lemming

Lemmus sibericus

Contrary to popular belief, lemmings do not commit suicide. During favourable years, the lemmings' ability to reproduce very quickly leads to population explosions of amazing proportions. As the population size goes up, space becomes more and more difficult to find, and young are pushed away from the best habitat, down the mountains and into the valleys.

Lemmings are good swimmers when they have to be, but they don't know their limits. During dispersal, youngsters often try to cross large bodies of water, drowning in the process. It is this behaviour which gave rise to the misconception that they kill themselves.

During the summer, lemmings spend much of their time underground in burrows, but when the ground starts to freeze in autumn, the lemmings cannot dig through the ground and are forced to forage on the surface. The lemmings do not hibernate during the harsh Scandinavian winter, but construct tunnel systems under the snow in search of food. The tunnels keep them out of sight from hungry predators, such as great grey owls, which are heavily reliant on lemmings as a source of food.

Unlike other species of lemming, the Siberian lemming does not change the colour of its coat in winter.

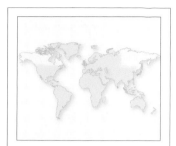

Distribution: Siberia and northern North America.
Habitat: Tundra grassland.
Food: Moss and grass.
Size: 13–18cm (5–7in); 23–34g (0.05–0.07lb).
Maturity: 5–6 weeks.
Breeding: These prolific breeders may produce 8 litters of up to 6 young each throughout the summer.
Life span: Less than 2 years.
Status: Common.

Alpine marmot (*Marmota marmota*): 45–60cm (18–24in); 3–4.5kg (6.5–10lb)
Alpine marmots live in the alpine and subalpine pastures of the Alps. Like many other marmots, alpine marmots live in family groups, consisting of a breeding pair and their offspring from previous years. Older male offspring are known to help keep their younger siblings warm during the cold alpine winters. Litter sizes tend to be small – about two pups. The pups stay with their parents until they are three years old.

Southern birch mouse (*Sicista subtilis*): 5–9cm (2–3.5in); 6–14g (0.015–0.03lb)
These tiny mice inhabit the forests, moors, meadows and steppes of eastern Europe and Asia. They excavate shallow burrows, in which they build oval-shaped nests of dry grass and cut plant stems. They travel over the ground in leaps and bounds. They are also great climbers. Strong outer toes grip twigs, and their prehensile tail curls around other branches for additional support.

Common hamster (*Cricetus cricetus*): 20–27cm (8–11in); 200–500g (0.45–1.1lb)
The stocky common hamster feeds on cereal crops, potatoes and beets, and also on small birds and other rodents when it has the chance. It makes large stockpiles of food within its large burrow system, which is dug in the ground and has an intricate network of tunnels. Food, intended for storage, is carried back home in its cheek pouches. Its range extends from western Europe to central Russia. Females often produce 2 litters of 6–12 young during summer.

House mouse

Mus musculus

The key to the house mouse's phenomenal success as a species is its ability to follow humans around the globe, and the way it is able to make use of whatever food sources people provide. By stowing away on ships and, latterly, aeroplanes, house mice have been able to colonize every continent of the world.

Mice were first domesticated, and in some instances worshipped, by the Romans and ancient Greeks. However, these days house mice are considered to be a major pest. They cause billions of dollars' worth of damage to food stores worldwide every year. They also damage buildings, woodwork, furniture and clothing, and are known to carry various dangerous diseases, including typhus and salmonella.

However, house mice are virtually unrivalled in their capacity to adapt to new surroundings. Their generalist habits, rapid breeding rate and talent for slipping into places unnoticed has enabled mice to become possibly the most numerous mammal in the world today.

A common sight all over the world, the house mouse is capable of making the most of any opportunity.

Distribution: Every continent of the world, including Antarctica.
Habitat: Generally near human habitation.
Food: Virtually anything.
Size: 15–19cm (6–7.5in); 17–25g (0.04–0.05lb).
Maturity: 5–7 weeks.
Breeding: Usually around 5–10 litters of 3–12 offspring during the year.
Life span: 12–18 months.
Status: Abundant.

Cape porcupine

Hystrix africaeaustralis

The Cape porcupine shares its habitat with a whole array of dangerous predators, but its sharp quills can repel even lions and hyenas. A mane of long, white bristles runs down the neck to the back. The rodent has special hollow quills attached to its tail, which can be rattled together as a warning to any unsuspecting animal that gets too close for comfort. Covering the lower back are 40cm (16in) long quills, equipped with tiny barbs. These quills are only loosely held in the skin and will embed themselves easily into any animal attempting to attack. Porcupines have keen hearing and an excellent sense of smell, which they use to locate nutritious bulbs underground. The Cape porcupines, like other rodents, also chew bones from carcasses to obtain calcium, phosphorus and other essential minerals. Chewing bones also helps to keep their incisor teeth sharp. Porcupines will often share burrows, forming clans comprising adult pairs and up to four offspring of varying ages. Members of the clan share common runs, trails and latrines, and also common feeding sites and refuges.

The Cape porcupine has the longest quills of any species of porcupine in the world.

Distribution: Widespread in Africa south of the Sahara Desert.
Habitat: Grassland.
Food: Roots, bark, herbs and fruit.
Size: 0.7–1m (2.25–3.25ft); up to 17kg (37.5lb).
Maturity: 9 months.
Breeding: Mated females produce up to 2 offspring at a time.
Life span: Up to 20 years.
Status: Endangered in some parts of its range, but common elsewhere.

Red squirrel

Sciurus vulgaris

Red squirrels can be quite variable in colour, with some individuals being jet black, while others are strawberry blonde. The bushy tail helps them to balance in the treetops. These arboreal rodents are very acrobatic.

The red squirrel has undergone a well-documented decline in Britain due to its not being able to compete with the larger and more robust grey squirrel, which was introduced from North America. The two species actually hardly ever come to blows, and it is thought that the main problem may be that the grey squirrels harbour a viral infection that decimates red squirrels whilst leaving the greys unaffected.

Red squirrels tend to be most active during early mornings and late afternoons. They rest in the middle of the day. As winter sets in, the squirrels rapidly put on weight, and settle down for a long period of inactivity. Squirrels do not truly hibernate. They never let their body temperatures drop, and they regularly wake up to stretch their legs, drink and feed from food caches made in the autumn.

Red squirrels are mainly solitary animals, and apart from when there is a large concentration of food, the only time they get together in any numbers is when the females become ready to breed. Males fight over them at this time.

Distribution: Europe and Asia.
Habitat: Primarily coniferous forests.
Food: Seeds and nuts when available, and also fungi, eggs, flowers and tree sap.
Size: 25–35cm (10–14in); up to 350g (0.75lb).
Maturity: 9–10 months.
Breeding: 2 litters of 5–7 young per year.
Life span: 4–6 years.
Status: Rare in the UK, common elsewhere.

Naked mole rat

Heterocephalus glaber

Naked mole rats live in societies which are more like social insects' colonies than those of other mammals. They live an entirely underground existence, and colonies can occupy 4km (2.5 miles) of tunnels, which are dug out by the rodents' claws and incisors. Some of these tunnels run just beneath the surface of the ground; others descend up to a 2m (80in) depth.

Like colonies of bees and ants, naked mole rat colonies are governed by queens, which give birth to the young. The queens are the largest individuals in the colonies, which usually comprise around 70 animals, but can number 300. The other individuals – the workers and drones – are separated into castes depending on their size. The members of each different caste have their own particular jobs, for example foraging, tunnel maintenance, caring for the young or nest defence.

Naked mole rats are the only mammals that have lost the ability to produce their own body heat. Instead, they bask in shallow tunnels warmed by the sun, or huddle together to keep warm.

As their name suggests, naked mole rats are almost hairless, with the pinkish skin showing through. They use their strong incisors and large claws for digging tunnels. These rodents are virtually blind.

Distribution: Kenya, Ethiopia and Somalia.
Habitat: Underground in arid savannah and grassland.
Food: Underground parts of plants, particularly the succulent tubers.
Size: 6–10cm (2.4–4in); 25–70g (0.05–0.15lb).
Maturity: 1 year.
Breeding: Usually about 12 young per litter, with 8 litters per year.
Life span: Over 20 years.
Status: Common.

Lord Derby's flying squirrel (*Anomalurus derbianus*): 27–38cm (11–15in); 0.5–1kg (1.1–2.2lb)
Belonging to an unusual group of rodents from central Africa known as scaly-tailed squirrels, these creatures glide from tree to tree. They leap into the air with their arms, legs and tails extended, stretching out membranes of skin that allow them to glide, but not fly, up to 250m (830ft). The scales on their tails are used as anchor-brakes, preventing them from skidding when they land on the trunks of trees.

North African gundi (*Ctenodactylus gundi*): 16–20cm (6.5–8in); 175–195g (0.3–0.4lb)
Found in the arid areas of northern Africa, gundis are small diurnal rodents that have very short legs, flat ears, big eyes and long whiskers. To warm up in the morning, they sit crouched on sunny rocks. When the wind is blowing through their fur, they have been said to resemble face-powder puffs.

Great cane rat (*Thryonomys swinderianus*): 35–61cm (14–24in); 3.5–4.5kg (7.5–10lb)
Great cane rats are large rodents that live in groups comprising one male, several females and the young from previous litters. They are nocturnal, and create trails through grass and reeds that lead from shelter to feeding and watering sites. They pound down tall grasses to make nests and also make shallow burrows for shelter. They are good swimmers and divers. If great cane rats become afraid, they either stomp their hind feet and grunt, or quickly run towards water.

Springhare

Pedetes capensis

Hopping is a very efficient way to travel, and it allows springhares to bound rapidly around the African savannah at night. Usually they do not move too far from their burrows, but during times of drought they have been known to travel up to 40km (25 miles) in search of water.

Springhares have incredibly keen senses. As well as having fantastic sight, scent and hearing, they use their huge back feet to pick up vibrations from the earth.

Springhares need all their senses to be able to avoid the long list of predators that would happily make meals of them. They are small enough to be manageable for wild cats, jackals, ratels and large owls, but big enough to interest larger predators, such as lions and leopards, should they get close enough to be able to catch them.

Rather like a small kangaroo, the bizarre springhare is in a family all of its own.

Distribution: Southern and eastern Africa.
Habitat: Grasslands with sandy soil.
Food: Vegetation, mainly bulbs and grasses.
Size: 35–45cm (14–18in); 4kg (8.8lb).
Maturity: 1 year.
Breeding: Around 3 or 4 young per litter, with litters born about every 100 days.
Life span: 10 years.
Status: Common and widespread.

BATS

With nearly 1,000 species, bats form one of the largest groups among the mammals, living in almost all temperate and tropical parts of the world. They are the only mammals to have truly mastered flight, and more than half of the species are known to use echolocation for navigating and capturing prey at night. Different bats are specialized for eating insects, fruit, flowers, blood, fish and small animals.

Greater mastiff bat

Mops condylurus

This species is also known as the Angolan free-tailed bat, reflecting the disagreement in its classification. Some scientists place the greater mastiff bat in the same group as the free-tailed bats, while others place it in a separate group.

The greater mastiff bat roosts in caves, mines, hollow trees and can even be found under thatched roofs and in attics. The bats form groups of several hundred individuals. At sundown they fly out of their roosts to hunt insects. A colony of 500 individuals can consume a tonne of insects per year, and ecologists are thinking of using these bats to control insect pests in Africa, such as mosquitoes that carry malaria. Scientists have started designing artificial roosts or bat "hotels" to encourage the bats to feed in areas where insect pests breed. While designing the artificial roosts, researchers discovered that the bats are capable of tolerating up to 45°C (113°F) during the heat of tropical midday.

This bat is characterized by having wrinkly lips and a band of skin joining the ears, over the top of its head.

Distribution: Africa south of the Sahara Desert, including Madagascar.
Habitat: Forest, savannah and dry brushland.
Food: Insects.
Size: 5–6cm (2–2.5in); 7–64g (0.015–0.15lb).
Maturity: 3 months.
Breeding: 2 breeding seasons per year, with a single young produced per season.
Life span: Not known.
Status: Not included in IUCN Red List.

Hammer-headed fruit bat

Hypsignathus monstrosus

This is the largest bat in Africa, and is remarkable in having the greatest difference between males and females (sexual dimorphism) of any bat species. Males are nearly twice as heavy as females and, unlike females, they have an unusually large square-shaped head, giving the species its name. The male head-shape is one of several adaptations for calling, which include a greatly enlarged voice box, allowing males to produce a continuous and very loud croaking and quacking, probably to attract females.

Twice a year, male hammer-headed fruit bats congregate into groups of up to 130 individuals, in order to compete for mates. The males attract attention by croaking as loudly as possible and flapping their wings. The females are very selective, and most opt to mate with just a few of the noisiest males. When the bats are not breeding, they roost quietly during the day in small groups high up in the treetops. At night, hammer-headed bats fly up to 10km (6 miles) from their roost sites to find trees with ripened fruit to eat.

The male's head is large and square, and the muzzle is hammer-shaped. The males also have large lips and warty snouts. Females have thinner, fox-like muzzles.

Distribution: Central and western Africa.
Habitat: Forests, swamps, mangroves and river margins.
Food: Fruit, and also reported to have killed and eaten tethered chickens.
Size: Up to 0.9m (36in); up to 0.5kg (1.1lb).
Maturity: Females 6 months; males 18 months.
Breeding: Give birth to single young, or sometimes twins, once or twice per year.
Life span: Not known.
Status: Common.

Little flying cow (*Nanonycteris veldkampi*): 5–7.5cm (2–3in); 19–33g (0.04–0.07lb)
This small flower-feeding bat can be found in parts of western and central Africa. It gets its curious name from the apparently calf-like appearance of its head. This species migrates from forests to savannahs during the rainy season.

Butterfly bat (*Glauconycteris variegata*): 35–65mm (1.5–2.5in); 6–14g (0.01–0.03lb)
This African bat gets its name from its beautifully patterned wings and butterfly-like flight, and can be found roosting in small groups under palm fronds or banana leaves. Butterfly bats feed on small insects, sometimes foraging in broad daylight.

Long-tailed bat (*Rhinopoma microphyllum*): 5–9cm (2–3.5in); 6–14g (0.01–0.03lb)
This species has a tail nearly as long as its body, and lives in dry, treeless regions in northern and western Africa, parts of the Middle East and southern India. Long-tailed bats can often be found roosting in houses, and in Egypt they are believed to have roosted in the great pyramids for thousands of years.

Noctule bat

Nyctalus noctula

The noctule bat is one of the largest and most common European bats. In winter, noctules roost in hollow trees or old woodpecker holes, and occasionally in buildings. In some parts of Europe, groups of 1,000 individuals may roost together.

Noctules hunt insects in flight, and are capable of flying at speeds of 50kph (30mph) or more. Usually they forage at dusk, catching insects over woodland or close to water, and sometimes they are seen hunting insects that gather around street lamps in towns.

Although noctules are capable of surviving in cold conditions without food for up to four months, they also migrate to warmer areas where there is more food. Noctules have been known to migrate as far as 2,347km (1,455 miles). In late summer, solitary male noctules set up breeding roosts in tree holes, attracting up to 20 females with mating calls and pheromones. In early summer, pregnant females form groups of related individuals, then they help one another nurse their young.

Distribution: Europe to Japan.
Habitat: Forests.
Food: Insects, especially beetles, and also midges and moths.
Size: 32–40cm (12–16in); 15–40g (0.03–0.08lb).
Maturity: Females 3 months; males 1 year.
Breeding: Single litter of 1, 2 or occasionally 3 young born per year.
Life span: 12 years.
Status: Declining in some parts of its range.

The colour of the noctule bat ranges from a golden brown to a dark brown on the back, usually with paler brown coloration on the belly.

Pipistrelle bat

Pipistrellus pipistrellus

These small bats are common throughout most of Europe, but have declined in some countries due to the loss of natural roosting sites in trees. The reduction is also due to toxic chemicals that have been used to treat wood in the buildings where many pipistrelles roost during winter time. In some parts of Europe, pipistrelles hibernate in winter, either individually or in groups, hidden in crevices in buildings and trees. However, very cold weather may force wintering pipistrelles to move to warmer areas.

Mating usually takes place in autumn, when the bats congregate at traditional breeding roosts. Females give birth to their young in summer, when they come together in large maternity colonies to suckle and care for them.

Pipistrelles leave their roosts early in the evening to feed, chasing after insects in a characteristic fast and jerky pursuit flight, using echolocation. A single pipistrelle can eat as many as 3,000 insects in one night. Usually the high-pitched squeaks that pipistrelles make for echolocation are inaudible to humans, but some people can hear the lower-frequency parts of their calls.

There are two subspecies of pipistrelle bat, distinguished by the pitch of their calls. One is known as the tenor, while the other is the soprano. The largest colonies may number many thousands.

Distribution: Europe, North Africa, south-western and central Asia, and possibly Korea and Japan.
Habitat: Forests, farmland, wetlands and urban habitats, nesting in lofts.
Food: Insects.
Size: Wingspan 19–25cm (7.5–10in); 3–8g (0.006–0.017lb).
Maturity: Females 6 months; males 1 year.
Breeding: 1 young or occasionally twins produced per year.
Life span: 16 years.
Status: Common.

AARDVARK AND PANGOLIN

Recent scientific work has shown that, although the aardvark and pangolin share some superficial resemblance and behaviour, they do not have common ancestry. Indeed, they are now placed in separate groups. It is perhaps not surprising that specialist ant-eating mammals evolved independently several times, given the abundance of ants and termites found in almost all habitats around the world.

Aardvark

Orycteropus afer

Distribution: Sub-Saharan Africa.
Habitat: Woodland, savannah, grassland and shrubland.
Food: Ants, termites, other insects, small mammals and vegetable material.
Size: 1–1.5m (3.25–5ft); 40–70kg (88–154lb).
Maturity: 2 years.
Breeding: 1 or occasionally 2 young per year.
Life span: 20 years.
Status: Common.

These animals are often found foraging out in the open at night, systematically covering the ground in search of ants or termites. Aardvarks travel long distances in looking for food, often travelling 10km (6 miles) in a single night. Not surprisingly, given their long tubular ears and snout, they have acute hearing and a good sense of smell with which to detect their prey. They use their powerful front claws to dig open ant and termite nests, and their long sticky tongues to collect the insects. These animals have very thick skin, and seem to be immune to insect bites.

The aardvark's skin is so tough that it also saves it from bites by predators. Aardvarks are very well adapted for digging. When alarmed, they will either run away or start digging a burrow. A single aardvark can dig a hole faster than several people using shovels. Temporary aardvark burrows are less than 3m (10ft) deep, with end chambers large enough for the animals to turn in. More permanent burrows can be 13m (42ft) long with several chambers and entrances.

The word aardvark means "earth-pig" in Afrikaans, reflecting both the burrowing habits and pig-like features of this unusual animal. It has long ears, an elongated snout, a shaggy body and powerful tail. It folds its ears back while making its burrows.

Cape pangolin

Manis temmincki

There are four species of pangolin, also known as scaly anteaters, living in Africa. Two of them are tree-living animals with long prehensile tails, which they use when climbing. The other two species, which include the endangered Cape pangolin, live in burrows and forage on the ground.

Pangolins feed solely on ants and termites. They have several adaptations, such as having no teeth, which help them in this regard. Like other ant-eating mammals, they have sticky tongues up to 25cm (10in) long for collecting their prey, and strong claws to tear open termite nests. Unlike any other mammals, however, pangolins have scales rather than hairs, giving them a reptilian appearance. When a pangolin is threatened, it rolls up into a tight ball, protecting its soft underparts and presenting a formidable, scaly barrier to predators. The Cape pangolin has declined in numbers because, like its Asian cousins, it is in demand for its scales, which are used in local medicines.

Pangolins usually walk on their knuckles to save wear and tear on their claws, which they use for opening ant and termite nests. Sometimes they walk on their back legs, using the trailing tail to keep balance.

Distribution: Chad and Sudan to Namibia and South Africa.
Habitat: Savannah and shrubland.
Food: Ants, termites and occasionally other insects.
Size: 40–50cm (16–20in); 15–18kg (33–40lb).
Maturity: 2 years.
Breeding: 1 or occasionally 2 young.
Life span: Not known.
Status: Threatened.

ELEPHANTS AND RELATIVES

There are only two living species of elephant: African and Indian. Extinct species include the woolly mammoth and pygmy elephant. Although there is some disagreement among scientists, the closest relatives of the elephants are thought to be sea cows and hyraxes, neither of which bear much resemblance to elephants. However, similarities in their DNA codes reveal their shared ancestry.

African elephant

Loxodonta africana

There are two races of African elephants: the savannah elephant, which is the world's largest living land animal, and the smaller forest elephant that lives in the rainforests of central and western Africa. The savannah elephants are social animals and, like Indian elephants, they form groups consisting of related female elephants and their young.

The leaders of elephant groups are always the eldest and largest females. Male elephants leave their groups at puberty, driven away by older females, to go and join groups of other young males. Males compete to mate, and usually these contests are settled by pushing and aggressive displays, but sometimes fighting leads to fatal injuries.

Forest elephants do not form large groups, but are able to maintain contact with other elephants in the dense jungle by producing deep, rumbling calls.

One of the most distinctive features of an elephant is its trunk. It is a very adaptable tool, and can be used for picking up anything from peanuts to trees. It is used for feeding, drinking, fighting and communication.

Distribution: Sub-Saharan Africa.
Habitat: Forest, savannah, marshland and semi-desert.
Food: Grass, leaves, shrubs, bark, twigs, roots and fruit.
Size: 6–7.5m (20ft–25ft), up to 7.5 tonnes (16,500lb).
Maturity: 10–20 years.
Breeding: Single calf born every few years.
Life span: 50–70 years.
Status: Endangered.

Rock hyrax

Procavia capensis

These small rodent-like animals live in groups in rocky areas, where there are plenty of nooks and crannies in which to hide. Hyraxes are surprisingly agile, and can run up even the steepest, smooth rock surfaces with ease, gripping the rocks with the rubber-like soles of their feet. Hyraxes have many enemies, which include leopards, eagles and pythons, so they have to be quick and watchful. In fact, the dominant male of a family group, which typically consists of several females and young, and sometimes a subordinate male as well, usually stands guard while the rest of the group feeds or basks in the sun. If the sentry animal spots danger, he will warn the rest of the group with an alarm call, signalling them to scamper off and hide in their burrows or between rocks.

Rock hyraxes don't like cold or wet weather, and will stay in their burrows if it is raining. When it is cold, groups of up to 25 animals will huddle together in a shelter to keep warm. On warm days, they come out to feed or bask in the sun. Hyraxes only come out at night if the weather is warm and there is plenty of moonlight, otherwise they stay in their burrows until daytime.

Rock hyraxes will eat almost any type of vegetation, even plant species poisonous to other mammals.

Distribution: Most of Africa, excluding the north-western regions.
Habitat: Rocky scrubland.
Food: Grass, leaves and shrubs.
Size: 30–58cm (12–23in); 4kg (9lb).
Maturity: 16–17 months.
Breeding: Litter of 1–6 young.
Life span: 11 years.
Status: Common.

HOOFED ANIMALS

This large group of plant-eating mammals is divided into two main groups, depending on whether they have an odd or even numbers of toes. They range in size from the tiny mouse deer, weighing less than 1kg (2lb) to the massive rhinoceroses and hippopotamuses that can weigh several tonnes. Hoofed animals are important for humans, having been domesticated as work animals and to provide food and clothing.

Dromedary camel

Camelus dromedarius

Distribution: North Africa to western India.
Habitat: Deserts and scrubland.
Food: Vegetation and carrion.
Size: 2.2–3.5m (7.25–11.5ft); 300–690kg (660–1500lb).
Maturity: 3 years.
Breeding: Single young or twins every 2 years.
Life span: 50 years.
Status: Common.

These tough animals have been domesticated in and around the Arabian peninsula for more than 4,000 years, and are prized for their endurance in hot, dry conditions. The dromedary, or one-humped camel, can carry loads of more than 200kg (440lb) for several days.

Camels can survive for long periods without drinking water. However, when water is available they can drink up to 57 litres (12 gallons) at a time to restore normal levels of body fluids. Camels have almost no sweat glands, so they lose water much more slowly than other mammals. Contrary to popular belief, the camel's hump contains fat, not water, and serves as an energy reserve – although the blubber does hold some water. During the breeding season, dominant males defend groups of up to 30 adult females from other males. Younger males form groups of bachelor males.

As well as its characteristic hump, camels have other adaptations to the harsh conditions of the desert, including broad feet for walking on loose sand, long eyelashes, hairy ears, and nostrils that can be closed to keep out sand and dust.

Common zebra

Equus burchelli

The common or Burchell's zebra has the broadest stripes of the three zebra species, and its stripes usually meet under the belly.

There are three different species of zebra, all found in Africa and each with its own distinctive pattern of black and white stripes. The stripes make these hoofed mammals blend into the natural patterns of light and shade in their habitat, making it more difficult for a predator to keep track of its quarry during a chase, especially when the zebras are running in a herd formation.

Zebras usually live in small family groups headed by dominant stallions, which lead groups of one to six mares with their young. When young male zebras reach maturity, they leave their family groups and form groups of bachelor males, while females stay behind. Males fight amongst each other for access to females, circling and trying to kick or bite one another. Within a group, zebras can be affectionate, and may spend a lot of time grooming one another.

Distribution: Ethiopia to southern Africa.
Habitat: Grassland and open woodland.
Food: Grass, herbs and leaves.
Size: 2.2–2.5m (7.25–8.25ft); 290–340g (640–750lb).
Maturity: 3 years.
Breeding: Single foal born every 1–2 years.
Life span: Up to 40 years in captivity.
Status: Declining, but unlike other zebras, not present on the IUCN Red List.

Giraffe

Giraffa camelopardalis

Giraffes are the world's tallest living land mammals, with some exceeding 5m (16.5ft) from top to toe. The giraffe's long neck has the same number of vertebrae as other mammals, but each one is greatly elongated. The giraffe's great height is an adaptation for feeding on young leaves in the upper branches of trees, which other browsing mammals cannot reach.

Giraffes have excellent sight, and because of their height they have the greatest range of vision of any terrestrial animal. If a giraffe spots danger, it will run away at speeds of up to 56kph (34mph). Occasionally, a giraffe will face its attacker, striking out with its front hooves or swinging its head like a club.

In order to reach fresh grass or drinking water, giraffes must splay their front legs apart, so that they can get their heads down to ground level. Giraffes settle on to their withdrawn legs to rest, and lie down when sleeping, resting their heads back on their hindquarters.

In times gone by, giraffes could be found in parts of North Africa, but due to a combination of over-hunting and the effects of climate change on vegetation, they are now only thinly distributed south of the Sahara Desert.

Distribution: Sub-Saharan Africa.
Habitat: Open woodland and savannah.
Food: Leaves, grass and grains.
Size: 5.9m (19.5ft); 550–1,930kg (1,200–4,200lb).
Maturity: Females 3.5 years; males 4.5 years.
Breeding: Usually 1 young born every 2 years.
Life span: Up to 26 years recorded in the wild, and 36 years recorded in captivity.
Status: Conservation-dependent.

Giraffes have prehensile lips and long tongues to help them gather leaves. They also have short horn-like ossicones on their heads – a feature they share with okapis.

Donkey (*Equus asinus*): 2m (6.5ft); 260kg (550lb)
This species was originally found wild in North Africa and the Middle East, but now occurs around the world as a domestic animal. Although much slower than horses, donkeys are very strong and they are capable of enduring harsh conditions.

Ibex (*Capra ibex*): 1.1–1.7m (3.5–5.5ft); 35–150kg (77–330lb)
A relative of the domestic goat, the ibex lives in Alpine regions of Europe, parts of the Middle East, north-eastern Africa, and some mountainous regions of Asia. The ibex has massive, curved horns that can be over half the length of the animal's body in males. The coat is grey-brown. Older males have a small beard and a "mane" of longer hairs on the back of the neck. It is threatened with extinction in some parts of its range.

Okapi

Okapia johnstoni

The okapi is a close relative of the giraffe. Although okapis are nowhere near as tall as giraffes, they do have relatively long necks and legs. Females are usually larger than males. Okapis have a deep red-brown coloration with distinctive horizontal black and white stripes along their rumps and legs. Despite their large size and unique appearance, they were not known to science until 1900.

Okapis spend most of their time alone, and they are very wary, running into dense cover if they detect danger. Sometimes okapis form small family groups and communicate with vocalizations and mutual grooming.

It is thought that there are between 10,000 and 20,000 okapis in the wild, but their dense forest habitat makes it very difficult for scientists to estimate their true population status.

Male okapis have small, hair-covered, horn-like ossicones. They also have very long tongues, capable of reaching their eyes.

Distribution: Congo Region.
Habitat: Dense tropical forest.
Food: Leaves, twigs and fruit.
Size: 1.9–2.1m (6–7ft); 200–300kg (440–660lb).
Maturity: Females reach sexual maturity at 1.5 years; males probably do not have the opportunity to mate until older.
Breeding: Single offspring born after a gestation of 421–427 days.
Life span: 30 years.
Status: Threatened.

Black rhinoceros

Diceros bicornis

The black rhino can be distinguished from Africa's second rhino species, the white rhino, by its pointed, prehensile upper lip, as compared to the white rhino's squared, non-prehensile upper lip. Despite the names, there is no colour difference between them.

The black rhinoceros is the smaller and more abundant of the two species of rhino found in Africa, but it is still critically endangered. These animals form clans that sometimes come together at wallowing sites, where they have mud baths. The baths help to keep the skin healthy and free of parasites. Rhinos within a clan are usually tolerant of each other, though occasionally serious fights may occur between bulls that are courting the same female.

Black rhinoceroses can be quite dangerous. They have very bad eyesight and may charge at anything large enough to be a threat, including vehicles, tents and campfires. However, they usually run away when they detect the scent of humans. Indeed, rhinos have good reason to fear humans. Hunting has destroyed the populations of both of the African species. People have hunted the rhino for sport, for its tough hide, but mostly for its horn. A rhino's horn is made from the same material as hair, and can be carved into ornamental objects or ground into medicinal or aphrodisiac powders. Many countries have banned trade in rhino products, but illegal trading still occurs.

Distribution: Eastern and southern Africa from southern Chad and Sudan to South Africa.
Habitat: Scrubland and woody savannah.
Food: Twigs and leaves.
Size: 3–3.75m (10–12.25ft); 800–1,400kg (1,760–3,080lb).
Maturity: Females 4–6 years; males 7–9 years.
Breeding: Single calf born every 2–5 years.
Life span: Can exceed 45 years in captivity.
Status: Critically endangered.

Hippopotamus

Hippopotamus amphibius

These enormous animals spend much of their time in water, where they keep cool out of the hot sun and take the weight off their legs. Hippopotamuses lie in the water with only their nostrils, eyes and ears above the surface, and they can also submerge for up to 30 minutes, while walking on the bottom of the river or lake. At night they leave their watery refuge in search of grass, sometimes travelling more than 3km (2 miles) from water.

Large males set up territories along riverbanks, which they defend against other males. Although neighbouring territory-holders are usually peaceful, confrontations sometimes occur. When this happens, the males challenge each other with displays, including lunging, splashing, scattering dung with their short tails and displaying their tusks with great yawns of their mouths. If neither male backs off, fighting occurs, and sometimes they attack each other with their tusks – which can lead to fatal injuries. Males are usually aggressive towards any intruders into their territories, including young hippos. Females are aggressive when they have young, and many consider hippos to be among the most dangerous of African mammals.

Distribution: Most of Sub-Saharan Africa.
Habitat: Deep water near reeds or grassland.
Food: Grass.
Size: 2–5m (6.5–16.5ft); 1–4.5 tonnes (2,200–9,900lb).
Maturity: 6–14 years.
Breeding: Usually a single young born during rainy season, with 2 years between births.
Life span: 40 years.
Status: Common.

The hippo's tusks – actually its canine teeth – can weigh up to 3kg (6.5lb) each, and are used in fighting. There have been some reports of hippos overturning small boats and biting the occupants to death.

Warthog

Phacochoerus africanus

This species gets its name from the warty protuberances located on the sides of the head and in front of the eyes, found only in the males. These powerful animals have large heads in proportion to the rest of their bodies, and both males and females have sharp tusks.

Unlike most species of wild pig, warthogs are active during the day, except in areas where they are likely to be attacked by humans. There they change to a nocturnal lifestyle in order to avoid human contact. When sleeping or rearing young, warthogs take refuge in holes – often those made by aardvarks.

If attacked by predators such as hyenas or lions, warthogs flee to the nearest available hole, backing into it so that they can face their attackers with their vicious tusks. Warthogs sometimes come together in groups called sounders, usually numbering 4–16 individuals. Although they are fairly abundant throughout their range, people hunt warthogs for their meat and to stop them eating crops. This poses a threat to warthog populations.

In male warthogs, the upper tusks can exceed 60cm (24in) in length. However, it is the smaller and sharper lower tusks that are the warthog's main weapon. Curiously, warthogs kneel down to feed on grass and roots.

Distribution: Throughout Africa from Mauritania to Ethiopia, and southward to Namibia and eastern South Africa.
Habitat: Savannah and open woodland.
Food: Grass, roots, berries, and sometimes carrion.
Size: 0.9–1.5m (3–5ft); 50–150kg (110–330lb).
Maturity: 18–20 months.
Breeding: 1–8 young.
Life span: Can exceed 18 years in captivity.
Status: Abundant, but the subspecies *P. a. aeliani* is classified as endangered.

Pygmy hippopotamus
(*Hexaprotodon liberiensis*): 1.5–1.7m (5–5.5ft); 160–270kg (350–600lb)
This animal is found in hot lowland jungles in parts of West Africa, and although it looks like a miniature version of the hippopotamus, there are a number of notable differences. These include a more rounded head and eyes on the side, rather than the top of the head.

Giant forest hog (*Hylochoerus meinertzhageni*): 1.3–2.1m (4.25–7ft); 130–275kg (280–600lb)
These large wild pigs travel about their tropical forest habitats in groups, or sounders, of up to 20 individuals, led by old males. Males are aggressive, will charge intruding males, and have also been known to charge humans.

Bush pig (*Potamochoerus porcus*): 1–1.5m (3.25–5ft); 46–130kg (100–285lb)
These pigs have long pointed ears, long white whiskers, and white crests along their backs. They live in the jungles of West Africa, where they forage for a wide range of food types at night. Their numbers have increased, probably as a result of the reduction of leopard populations.

Wild boar

Sus scrofa

Although domestic pigs usually look quite different from wild boar, they are in fact the same species, and can readily interbreed. Wild boar live in groups called sounders, consisting of females and their young. The males live alone, but join sounders in the mating season, when they compete for access to females.

Male wild boar can be very aggressive. In Doñana National Park in Spain, they have been known to chase adult lynxes away from carrion. Wild boars sometimes construct shelters from cut grass, and female wild boars are the only hoofed animals that give birth and look after their young inside a crude nest.

These animals have an excellent sense of smell, and are able to sniff out nutritious tubers and roots underground, while they snuffle through the leaf litter. Foraging wild boars often leave telltale signs, frequently ploughing up large patches of soil. In some countries, where wild boar have been introduced, they have had a negative impact on local animals and plants, either by feeding on them directly, or by disturbing their habitats.

Only male wild boar have tusks, which are extended upper and lower canine teeth. Piglets have striped patterns, which they lose as they get older.

Distribution: Europe, North Africa and Asia.
Habitat: Forest and shrublands.
Food: Leaves, roots, fungi, small mammals and reptiles, eggs, carrion and manure.
Size: 0.9–1.8m (3–5.75ft); 40–350kg (88–770lb).
Maturity: 8–10 months.
Breeding: 1 litter of 1–12 young born annually.
Life span: 10 years.
Status: Common.

Dibatag (*Ammodorcas clarkei*): 1.5–1.7m (5–5.5ft); 22–35kg (50–77lb) Dibatags are beautiful antelopes which live in savannah habitats in Ethiopia and Somalia. They have very long, slender necks that are used to reach leaves on high branches. This species is now under threat of extinction due to poaching.

Roe deer (*Capreolus capreolus*): 0.9–1.5m (3–5ft); 15–50kg (33–110lb) This graceful deer is found over large parts of Europe, including Britain, where it lives in forests and on farmland. The smallest European deer, it lives alone or in small groups. Roe deer have adapted well to habitat changes, and have actually increased in number.

Mouse deer (*Hyemoschus aquaticus*): 60–85cm (24–34in); 7–15kg (15–33lb) This species is found in lowland forests in central and western Africa. Neither males nor females have antlers, but the males have enlarged canines, similar to those of musk deer.

Red deer (*Cervus elaphus*): 1.6–2.6m (5.25–8.5ft); 75–340kg (160–750lb) This species is found throughout Europe, temperate Asia, north-west Africa and North America. Adult males possess antlers that can span up to 1.7m (5.5ft) across, and are used as weapons during the rutting season.

Fallow deer

Dama dama

Fallow deer are easily distinguishable from other species of deer by their somewhat flattened antlers and spotted summer coats. In some places fallow deer live alone, while in others they come together to form small herds of up to 30 individuals.

Breeding behaviour is variable, and may depend on the distribution of food. In some places males come together and attempt to attract females with dance-like rituals and bellowing – a rut. In other places, males attempt to monopolize females by defending good feeding areas from other males. Fallow deer have been introduced to many new places, but their populations are falling because of hunting and climate change.

Distribution: Originally found around the Mediterranean and parts of the Middle East, but since introduced to other countries, including Britain and New Zealand.
Habitat: Wide variety of habitats, including open woodland, grassland and shrubland.
Food: Mostly grass, but also leaves and twigs.
Size: 1.3–1.7m (4.25–5.5ft); 40–100kg (88–220lb).
Maturity: Females around 16 months; males around 17 months.
Breeding: A single fawn born annually.
Life span: 20 years or more in captivity.
Status: Common, but is disappearing from its original range.

Only the males sport antlers, which can span 80cm (32in) from tip to tip. Adults shed and regrow their antlers every year.

Reindeer

Rangifer tarandus

The reindeer, also known as the caribou in North America, is the only deer species in which both males and females possess antlers. Herds are organized into hierarchies based on the size of the deers' bodies and antlers. Most herds make seasonal migrations, moving to where food is available. Northern populations often travel more than 5,000km (3,000 miles). During the migration, reindeer groups congregate into great herds of up to half a million individuals.

Reindeer have been domesticated for 3,000 years, and there are huge numbers in northern Siberia.

The antlers of males can exceed 1m (3.25ft). Reindeer hooves are broad and flat – an adaptation for walking on soft ground and deep snow.

Distribution: Greenland, Scandinavia, Siberia, Mongolia, north-eastern China, Alaska, Canada and northern USA.
Habitat: Arctic tundra, boreal forests and mountainous habitats.
Food: Plant material (especially new growth in spring), leaves, twigs and lichens.
Size: 1.2–2.2m (4–7.25ft); 60–318kg (130–700lb).
Maturity: 1.5–3.5 years.
Breeding: 1 fawn produced annually.
Life span: 15 years.
Status: Common.

Royal antelope (*Neotragus pygmaeus*): 50cm (20in); 2kg (4.4lb) This is one of the smallest hoofed animals in the world, and is often found in forest clearings in parts of West Africa. It is well camouflaged, but will make enormous bounds if spotted by predators, reportedly achieving leaps of up to 2.8 m (9ft).

Thomson's gazelle (*Gazella thomsoni*): 0.8–1.7m (2.5–5.5ft); 12–85kg (26–187lb) These attractive gazelles are found in the dry habitats of Sudan, Kenya and Tanzania. Like several other antelopes, they have a behaviour called stotting. When they spot predators stalking them, they make a series of curious jumps, thought to act as signals. This behaviour probably signals to the predators that they have been spotted and should not bother trying to chase the obviously agile gazelles.

Bongo (*Tragelaphus eurycerus*): 1.7–2.5m (5.5–8.25ft); 150–220kg (330–484lb) This forest-dwelling animal has a chocolate-brown coat with creamy vertical stripes down its flanks. It has large ears, an erect mane running from its shoulders to its rump, and twisted horns. The bongo population is in decline because of hunting and habitat loss.

Blue gnu

Connochaetes taurinus

The blue gnu, also known as the wildebeest, is one of the most abundant large mammals in Africa. There are thought to be 1.5 million migratory individuals in the Serengeti alone, forming the greatest concentration of wild grazing animals on Earth. Some herds stay in the same place; others are nomadic, constantly searching for new sources of food.

The males leave their herds when they are over a year old, forming groups of bachelors. At about three or four years old, males set up small territories which they defend from other males, and attempt to mate with females entering their areas. Mating activity is seasonal, and is usually timed so that the majority of calves are born close to the beginning of the rainy season, when new grass is plentiful.

Although populations have increased in the Serengeti, numbers have declined in other areas, such as south-west Botswana. There, competition with livestock and destruction of crops has prompted farmers to kill gnus and set up long fences to prevent them from migrating to wetlands when there are seasonal droughts.

Distribution: Southern Kenya and southern Angola to northern South Africa.
Habitat: Savannah.
Food: Grass and succulent plants.
Size: 1.5m (5ft); 118–275kg (260–600lb).
Maturity: Females 2–3 years; males 3–4 years.
Breeding: Usually a single calf born each year.
Life span: Up to 21 years in captivity.
Status: Abundant, but continuing survival is dependent on conservation efforts.

Gnus are named after the calls made by competing males – "genu". There are two species; this one is blue-grey, while the other is dark brown and black.

Impala

Aepyceros melampus

Like many other antelopes, impalas have pointed, spiralling horns. Both sexes are similarly coloured, with a white belly, chin and tail, and black-tipped ears.

Impalas are one of a number of antelopes that live on the African savannah. They are very quick and agile, and are capable of jumping high in the air, often clearing heights greater than 3m (10ft).

When conditions are harsh in the dry season, impalas come together in mixed herds, which may number in the hundreds, to search for food. During the more plentiful wet season, males and females separate into different groups, with males competing for territories. Successful males mark their territories with urine and faeces and then lure females into them with tongue-flashing displays. This signal has the effect of making the females group together as they pass through the displaying males. Non-resident males run away or flash their own tongues in defiance.

Distribution: Kenya and southern Angola to northern South Africa.
Habitat: Savannah and open woodland.
Food: Grass, and leaves from bushes and trees.
Size: 1.1–1.5m (3.5–5ft); females 40–45kg (88–99lb); males 60–65kg (132–143lb).
Maturity: 1 year.
Breeding: Single fawn born at a time.
Life span: 13 years.
Status: Common.

Arabian oryx

Oryx leucoryx

The Arabian oryx is the only oryx found outside Africa. It is adapted to survive in very arid country. By the early 1970s the Arabian oryx was thought to be extinct in the wild, due to excessive hunting throughout the early 20th century. At this time, the only herds existed in zoos around the world. However, a captive-breeding programme was started in the 1960s, and oryx have been reintroduced into the wild in Oman, Jordan and Saudi Arabia. Wild populations now number around 500 individuals.

Since dry habitats contain relatively little nourishing plant material, oryx must range over vast areas to obtain enough food. Oryx are surprisingly good at detecting rainfall from a great distance, and will move towards areas where rain is falling so that they can eat fresh plant growth and drink water.

When water is not available, they eat succulent foods, such as melons or bulbs, to get the moisture they need. Oryx live in groups of around ten individuals, either consisting of a dominant male and females, or of a group of young males. Although the oryx's exceptionally long and sharp horns are formidable weapons, most contests between males are settled by ritualized sparring.

Distribution: Originally in much of the Middle East, now only a few reserves in Oman, Jordan and Saudi Arabia.
Habitat: Dry habitats, including arid scrubland and deserts.
Food: Grass, shrubs, succulent fruit and bulbs.
Size: 1.5–2.3m (5–7.5ft); 100–210kg (220–462lb).
Maturity: 1–2 years.
Breeding: Single calf born.
Life span: 20 years.
Status: Endangered.

Oryx have striking black or brown markings on their heads and lower bodies, and very long, straight horns, up to 1.5m (5ft) in length.

Chamois

Rupicapra pyrenaica

Distribution: North-western Spain, Pyrenees and central Italy. *R. rupicapra* is more widespread from Europe to the Middle East.
Habitat: Alpine meadows.
Food: Herbs, flowers, lichen, moss and pine shoots.
Size: 0.9–1.3m (3–4.25ft); 24–50kg (53–110lb).
Maturity: 8–9 years.
Breeding: 1–3 young born in spring.
Life span: 22 years.
Status: Endangered.

There are two distinct species of chamois, both found in mountainous areas of Europe. They are both quite similar in appearance and behaviour, but this species – *Rupicapra pyrenaica* – has a more restricted distribution, is rarer than the other, and is now dependent on conservation efforts for its survival.

One of the reasons that chamois are rare is because they were hunted excessively for their meat – considered a delicacy in some regions – and for their hides, which was once made into high-quality leather for polishing glass and cars. Chamois are well adapted to living in mountainous habitats, and are very agile. When they are alarmed, they can bound up steep rocky slopes, and can leap almost 2m (6.5ft) straight up to get to inaccessible rocks.

Chamois live in small herds, usually consisting of females and their young. In autumn, males join the herds to compete for females, fighting each other with their sharp horns. Female herd members will often help one another. If a mother dies, other females will look after the young, and the animals are generally thought to take it in turns to stand guard while the rest of the herd feeds.

Chamois have long, thick fur to keep them warm in alpine conditions. Both males and females possess the distinctively slender, sharp horns, which are shaped like upside-down "J"s.

European bison

Bison bonasus

These large animals are now very rare, but like their close relatives the American bison, they used to be very abundant. European bison disappeared from western Europe by the late Middle Ages, and became extinct in eastern Germany by the 18th century. The main reason for this decline was the loss of their habitat and an increase in hunting as human populations rose across northern Europe. By the early 20th century, European bison could only be found in Poland, and by 1925 both populations were extinct. Since then, new populations have been established in these places from captive European bison in zoos.

In former times, European bison formed groups of hundreds of animals during migrations or in good feeding grounds. Nowadays groups are much smaller, consisting of a few related females and their young. During the mating season there is fierce competition over females, and males charge and clash heads.

European bison have slightly less shaggy manes than those of American bison, but they have more powerfully built hindquarters. Both males and females have horns.

Distribution: Originally found over large parts of Europe including England, but now restricted to eastern Europe.
Habitat: Forest and grasslands.
Food: Leaves, twigs, bark and grass.
Size: 2.1–3.5m (7–11.5ft); 350–1,000kg (770–2,200lb).
Maturity: 2–4 years.
Breeding: Single calf born every 1–2 years.
Life span: Up to around 20 years in the wild, and 40 years in captivity.
Status: Endangered.

African buffalo (*Syncerus caffer*): 2.1–3.4m (7–11.25ft); 300–900kg (660–1,980lb)
These formidable animals can be very aggressive, and have been known to inflict fatal injuries on lions. Accordingly, lions tend to be reluctant to tackle these large buffalo unless they are very hungry. African buffalo form herds of 50–500 individuals.

Addax (*Addax nasomaculatus*): 1.5–1.7m (5–5.5ft); 60–125kg (132–275lb)
This antelope is found in the Sahara Desert, and is well adapted to dry, hot conditions. It rarely drinks, and can obtain most of its moisture from the plants that it eats. It moves great distances in search of vegetation. This species is now endangered as a result of overhunting.

Sitatunga (*Tragelaphus spekei*): 1.1–1.7m (3.5–5.5ft); 50–125kg (110–275lb)
This African species of antelope is related to the kudu, but is unusual in its semiaquatic habits. It spends much of its time wading around in dense reed beds in swampy ground, and is a good swimmer. If threatened, it may hide underwater with only its nostrils above the surface.

Common eland

Taurotragus oryx

This is one of two species of eland, both of which occupy similar types of open savannah habitat. The eland is the largest of a number of related species, characterized by spiralling horns and vertical cream-coloured stripes along the flanks and haunches.

Elands occupy large home ranges, using different habitats at different times of the year, and can cover in excess of 220sq km (86sq miles) per year. Approximately 14,000 eland live in the Serengeti National Park in East Africa, where they form small herds, usually consisting of less than 25 animals.

Like many hoofed animals, eland males fight for dominance and the opportunity to mate with females. Competing males shove each other with locked horns, until one gives up and retreats. Elands are easily tamed and, due to their highly nutritious milk, tender meat and good-quality hides, people are trying to domesticate them on farms in Africa and Russia.

Male elands tend to be larger than females, but both sexes carry characteristic spiralling horns, which may be up to 1m (3.25ft) long.

Distribution: Southern and eastern Africa.
Habitat: Savannah and open woodland.
Food: Leaves and fruit.
Size: 1.8–3.4m (5.75–11.25ft); 400–1,000kg (880–2,200lb).
Maturity: Males 4 years; females 3 years.
Breeding: Single calf born.
Life span: 23 years.
Status: Conservation-dependent.

APES

There are four species of great ape: the orang-utan of South-east Asia and the chimpanzee, bonobo and gorilla of Africa. There are three races of gorilla, though it is not certain whether they are separate subspecies. The great apes are human being's closest animal relatives. Humans share 98 per cent of their genetic code with the great apes. Our common ancestor – Kenyapithecus – lived in Africa 15 million years ago.

Chimpanzee

Pan troglodytes

Distribution: Gambia to Uganda.
Habitat: Tropical forest and woody savannah.
Food: Fruit, leaves, flowers, bark, insects and animals.
Size: 1–1.7m (3.25–5.5ft); 26–70kg (57–154lb).
Maturity: Females 13 years; males 15 years.
Breeding: Single young born every 3–6 years.
Life span: Around 60 years.
Status: Endangered.

These intelligent, social animals are very closely related to human beings, and give us some indication of the kind of animal from which we evolved. Indeed, chimps have a number of characteristics that were once thought to be exclusively human. For example, they are able to construct and use simple tools – tasks that few other animals, except humans and orang-utans, are capable of. One tool commonly used by chimps is a probe, made of a thin twig stripped of leaves, which is inserted into termite nests to extract these insects, which are then eaten.

Chimps live in groups comprising 15–80 animals, which have complex social structures. The dominant males are not necessarily the biggest or strongest individuals, but the ones best able to recruit the most allies. Chimps are territorial, and neighbouring groups are often aggressive towards one another. Indeed, chimps share an unpleasant characteristic with humans: they go to war, and sometimes individuals of one group will hunt and kill members of a neighbouring group.

Chimpanzees are tool-users, and they are also skilled at communication, which they do with vocalizations and facial expressions.

Western-lowland gorilla

Gorilla gorilla gorilla

Currently, three different races of gorilla are recognized: the western-lowland gorilla, the eastern-lowland gorilla and the mountain gorilla. The western-lowland gorillas are separated from the nearest population of eastern-lowland gorillas by at least 1,000km (625 miles).

Western-lowland gorillas live in relatively small groups of only about six animals, lead by dominant males, or silverbacks – so-called because of the grey-white fur only found on the backs of older males. Although gorillas are large and extremely powerful, they are gentler than chimpanzees.

Gorilla groups tend to avoid one another although, on occasion, groups will meet amicably for a short time. Sometimes meetings are not peaceful, and a dominant silverback may respond to intruders by standing up, hooting and beating his chest with cupped hands, followed by a display of strength by breaking branches. This display may lead to an all-out attack.

The armspan of a gorilla is greater than its height – up to a huge 2.75m (9ft). This illustration shows a female with her young.

Distribution: South-eastern Nigeria, west-central and southern Cameroon, south-western Central African Republic, Guinea, Gabon and the Congo.
Habitat: Lowland tropical forests.
Food: Leaves and shoots.
Size: 1.25–1.75m (4–5.5ft); females 70–140kg (150–300lb); males 135–275kg (300–600lb).
Maturity: Females 7 years; males 15 years.
Breeding: Single young, or occasionally twins.
Life span: 50 years.
Status: Endangered.

Mountain gorilla

Gorilla gorilla beringei

Although there is doubt as to whether mountain gorillas constitute a separate subspecies, genetic analysis has shown that they are more closely related to the eastern-lowland gorillas than the western-lowland gorillas. Mountain gorillas tend to be larger, and have much longer and silkier fur, especially on their arms, than their lowland cousins. They also occupy a very different habitat, and are found almost exclusively in cold mountain rainforests of bamboo, at altitudes over 2,000m (6,666ft).

Scientists George Schaller and Dian Fossey, who spent many years living in close contact with mountain gorillas, studied these enigmatic animals in detail. They found that they live in relatively large groups of up to 30 individuals, and that they communicate with a wide range of calls.

Gorillas travel up to 1km (0.6 miles) in search of food each day, and build crude nests out of leafy branches, usually on the ground, where they sleep at night. Mountain gorillas are only found in the region of the Virunga volcanoes (two of which are active) and Bwindi Forest in Uganda. They number little more than 600 animals in the wild. Mountain gorillas have suffered heavily from poaching and accidental trapping.

The long, silky fur of the mountain gorilla helps to protect it from the freezing conditions sometimes found in its mountain habitat. This illustration shows a male silverback foraging for leaves.

Distribution: The Virunga volcanoes lying between Congo, Rwanda and Uganda.
Habitat: Montane forest and bamboo forest.
Food: Leaves and shoots.
Size: 1.5–1.8m (5–6ft); females 110–140kg (240–300lb); males 200–275kg (440–605lb).
Maturity: Females 7 years; males 15 years.
Breeding: Single young, or occasionally twins, born after 9 months' gestation. Females usually give birth to only 2–3 surviving young in a lifetime.
Life span: 50 years.
Status: Critically endangered.

Bonobo

Pan paniscus

Although commonly known as the pygmy chimpanzee, this species is often the same size as its close relative – *Pan troglodytes* – and is also very similar in appearance, though less powerfully built. Unlike chimpanzees, bonobos have never been observed to use tools in the wild, though in captivity they have been seen to use leaves to clean themselves, and sticks to pole-vault over water.

Bonobos are very social animals, and live in groups of 40–120 individuals. These groups move about by day searching for fruiting trees. When a food source is located, individuals make loud calls, probably to alert other members of their group and warn off members of other groups. Like chimps, bonobos construct temporary nests made from leafy branches, to sleep in at night.

Bonobo societies are much less aggressive than groups of chimps. Serious fighting is rare, and they never make deliberate lethal raids on neighbouring groups. Unlike chimp societies, females have equal ranking with males in bonobo groups, and form the cores of bonobo societies. A curious characteristic of bonobo behaviour is the use of sexual contact to settle arguments or to calm down aggressive situations.

Unlike in chimpanzee societies, it is frequently the females that adopt the leadership roles in bonobo groups.

Distribution: Central Congo.
Habitat: Lowland forests.
Food: Mostly fruit, occasionally leaves and seeds, rarely invertebrates and small vertebrates.
Size: 70–83cm (30–35in); 27–61kg (60–135lb).
Maturity: 9 years.
Breeding: Single young, or occasionally twins, born every 3–6 years after a gestation of 227–232 days.
Life span: Probably similar to that of the closely related chimpanzee.
Status: Endangered.

MONKEYS

There are nearly a hundred species of monkey found in the Old World (Africa and Eurasia). Old World monkeys belong to the family Cercopithecidae. *Most species of monkey are well adapted for life in trees and can move with great agility, jumping from branch to branch. Most monkeys live in tropical regions, where leaf and fruit production is year-round, providing these active animals with continuous food.*

Hamadryas baboon

Papio hamadryas

There are five species of baboon living in Africa, although some are known to be able to interbreed, leading some scientists to suggest that they are just different varieties or subspecies. If suitable resting sites are rare, hamadryas baboons can be found congregating in large groups, called troops, consisting of 100 or more individuals.

When baboons start looking for food in the morning, they split up into bands, each consisting of several groups of four or five females and young, led by a dominant male. When a female is ready to mate, the dominant male prevents other males from approaching, striking out when an intruder gets close. Sometimes young male baboons form temporary partnerships to defeat dominant males and get access to females. One of the pair distracts a dominant male by starting a fight with him, while the other mates. At a later time, the individuals in the partnership swap roles, and the one who had to fight last time will have the opportunity to mate.

Male hamadryas baboons have bright red faces and wild silvery hair. Females are smaller, sometimes only half the size of males, and have paler faces with brown hair.

Distribution: North-eastern Africa and western Arabian peninsula.
Habitat: Open woodland, savannah and rocky hill country.
Food: A wide range of plants and small animals.
Size: 61–76cm (24–30in); 14–41kg (30–90lb).
Maturity: Females 5 years; males 7 years.
Breeding: Single young.
Life span: 30 years.
Status: Threatened.

Mandrill

Mandrillus sphinx

This is the largest monkey in the world, with males weighing up to 54kg (120lb). The adult males are particularly colourful, with bright blue and purple nose ridges, scarlet noses and lilac buttock pads. There is a strong hierarchy among male mandrills, and it has been shown that the males with the most prominent facial coloration and the biggest rumps have the most success in attracting females and fathering young.

Mandrills move about in groups of up to ten adult females – with or without infants – around ten juveniles, and single dominant males.

Foraging mandrills cover around 8km (5 miles) per day. Usually the male stays close to the back of the group, but when there is danger he moves to the front to defend the group. Although mandrills are famous for their formidable appearance and ferocity, captive individuals are usually quite gentle.

A male mandrill's face is very brightly coloured, especially when he becomes excited. Females have duller, blue faces and are less heavily built than males.

Distribution: Southern Cameroon, Equatorial Guinea, Gabon and Congo.
Habitat: Dense lowland rainforest.
Food: Mostly fruit, nuts and other vegetable material, and also invertebrates and occasionally small mammals.
Size: 61–76cm (24–30in); 30–54kg (66–120lb).
Maturity: Females 3.5 years; males probably much older.
Breeding: Single young born each year.
Life span: 45 years.
Status: Threatened.

Vervet

Cercopithecus aethiops

Male vervets posses bright blue scrotums, which are used in signals of dominance over other males in a group.

Like many monkey species, vervets are very social, forming communicative groups of up to 50 individuals. These monkeys have a broad repertoire of calls, and are able to express alarm, excitement, rage and even sadness. Vervets forage in trees and occasionally on the ground. If predators are spotted, particular alarm calls are given, depending on the type of predator approaching. When vervets hear their snake alarm call, they all stand upright, scanning the surrounding grass for pythons. If they hear their leopard alarm call, they run into the trees, keeping their eyes on the leopard, and if they hear their eagle alarm call, they hide deep in the tree canopy.

Female vervets tend to remain in the groups into which they they were born, whereas males are forced to leave when they become sexually mature, moving into new groups. Vervets have adapted well to living alongside people. They are common in even the suburbs of big cities. Many people welcome their presence, but others treat them as pests because they can damage property and crops.

Distribution: Eastern and southern Africa.
Habitat: Riverine woodland, wooded savannah, open forests and agricultural land.
Food: Fruit and vegetable material, insects, crustaceans, birds' eggs and vertebrates.
Size: 35–66cm (14–27in); 2.5–9kg (5.5–20lb).
Maturity: Females 3 years; males 5 years.
Breeding: Usually a single young born each year.
Life span: 30 years.
Status: Common.

Barbary ape (*Macaca sylvanus*): 76cm (30in); 18kg (40lb)
Despite its name, this species is not actually an ape, but a macaque monkey. This is the only species of macaque living in Africa, and is also found on the Rock of Gibraltar, where it was introduced by the Romans. It is the only species of monkey living in the wild in Europe.

Gelada (*Theropithecus gelada*): 50–72cm (20–28in); females 14kg (30lb); males 20kg (44lb)
Geladas have long side whiskers, a mane of hairs on the neck, and three bare red patches of skin on the chest and throat. This is the only species of grazing monkey, and is found in very large groups in a small area in the mountains of central Ethiopia. It lives in rocky gorges where it can find sleeping sites and refuge from predators.

Guereza colobus monkey (*Colobus guereza*): 45–72cm (18–29in); 5–15kg (11–33lb)
There are five species of colobus monkey, and this one has a distinctive white beard and a face framed by white fur, a long white mantle, and a white tuft on the end of the tail, contrasting with the rest of its fur, which is black. Colobus monkeys have no thumbs.

Red-capped mangabey

Cercocebus torquatus

These monkeys are large and very vocal. Their calls can be heard from over 1km (0.6 miles) away. Groups of red-capped mangabeys consist of about 30 individuals, and unlike many species of monkey, their groups may include more than one adult male. All mangabeys have pale upper eyelids, which they flutter to attract attention and signal sexual intentions and status.

Although mangabeys spend a lot of time in the treetops searching for fruit, they will also forage on the ground, searching the leaf litter for mushrooms and small animal prey.

Mangabeys are territorial when food is relatively scarce in the dry season, and their loud calls help neighbouring groups maintain their distance from one another. At other times of the year, mangabey troops come together without conflict.

Mangabeys are threatened by the loss of their forests to logging. However, the red-capped mangabey seems to be quite adaptable to new habitats, hopefully making this species less susceptible.

Distribution: Senegal to Congo.
Habitat: Mostly tropical rainforest, but also mangroves, degraded forest, swamps and agricultural land.
Food: Mostly fruit, but other vegetable matter and insects and small animals are also taken.
Size: 38–89cm (15–35in); 7–14kg (15–30lb).
Maturity: Females 4 years; males 5–7 years.
Breeding: Single young, or occasionally twins, born at an average 16-month interval.
Life span: Probably around 30 years.
Status: Endangered.

The fur on the top of this species' head is a dark maroon-red. The white hair on the sides of the head extends around the neck like a collar, giving rise to the other common name of this species: the collared mangabey.

PRIMITIVE PRIMATES

This group includes some of the most specialized mammals in the world. They are referred to as primitive because they usually have much simpler social structures than other primates, and are more closely related to the insectivorous mammals from which all primates evolved. Also known as prosimians, primitive primates can be found in tropical regions of Africa, Asia and Madagascar.

Ruffed lemur

Varecia variegata

Distribution: Eastern Madagascar.
Habitat: Tropical forest.
Food: Fruit.
Size: 51–56cm (20–22in); 3.2–4.5kg (7–10lb).
Maturity: 2–3.5 years.
Breeding: 1–6 young, most commonly twins.
Life span: 33 years.
Status: Endangered.

This is the largest of all the lemurs. Lemurs are prosimians that are found exclusively on Madagascar and some surrounding islands. Ruffed lemurs live in trees, and although they are good climbers, they are not as agile as some other species of lemur.

Ruffed lemurs are most active at dusk, and at this time it is possible to hear their mournful territorial calls. Sometimes just a pair of ruffed lemurs occupies a territory, but more often groups of about 15 individuals will live together, sharing the same home range.

As well as calls, ruffed lemurs use scent-marking to signal their territorial boundaries. The males mark branches and other objects with a secretion from glands found on their necks. Scent-marking males are seen rubbing their chests, necks and chins on to trees or on the ground. Sadly, like many lemurs, these beautiful animals are in danger of extinction due to the overexploitation of their habitat and also overhunting of the animals themselves for their meat and fur, and for commercial exportation.

There are two subspecies of ruffed lemur. One has mostly black fur with white markings; the other has mostly red fur with white markings.

Indri

Indri indri

The indri is the largest of all the living prosimians, and like the lemurs, it is found only in Madagascar. Indris are arboreal and move about by jumping between tree trunks and stems. Sometimes indris come down to the ground, where they stand upright, moving in series of ungainly leaps.

They are mostly active by day and spend a lot of time feeding on leaves and fruit. Indris live in small family groups of up to five members, and occupy large home ranges. The central part of a home range is defended from others by the adult male, which uses scent markings and calls to signal the limits of the territory.

Sometimes several members of a group will make loud tuneful songs that can be heard up to 2km (1.25 miles) away. These songs are thought to signal occupancy of a territory to other groups, but also to unite groups and broadcast willingness to mate.

Indris have thick silky fur, which may be particularly useful for living in cold mountain forests, as high as 1800m (6000ft) above sea level. There is considerable variation in fur colour, which ranges from black through browns and greys to white.

Distribution: North-eastern Madagascar.
Habitat: Tropical rainforest.
Food: Leaves, flowers and fruit.
Size: 61–90cm (24–36in); 6–10kg (13–22lb).
Maturity: 7–9 years.
Breeding: Single young born every 2–3 years.
Life span: Not known.
Status: Endangered.

Aye aye

Daubentonia madagascariensis

This remarkable species is another prosimian found only in Madagascar. Aye ayes live alone. They are exclusively nocturnal and search for food high up in the trees, moving up to 4km (2.5 miles) a night within a small home range of around 5ha (12 acres). During the day, aye ayes sleep in spherical nests, made from branches and interwoven leaves. The nests are hidden in dense foliage in the forks of trees, and there may be several nests within a single home range.

Aye ayes have a most unusual way of finding food. Using a specially adapted finger, which is very long and thin like a probe, they tap the surface of decaying wood in search of tunnels made by insect larvae or ants and termites. Using a combination of a good sense of touch and a sort of echolocation with their sensitive ears – able to pinpoint a hollow sound from tapping – aye ayes locate the tunnels occupied by their prey. They then use their strong incisor teeth to make small holes in the wood, into which they insert their probe-like finger to extract their insect prey with a hooked claw. Unfortunately, these fascinating creatures are suffering from the loss of Malagasy forest. Local people also persecute them because they are seen as bad omens.

The aye aye not only uses its specialized third finger for locating and catching insects in decaying wood, but also for determining the milk content of coconuts and extracting coconut pulp.

Distribution: Northern, eastern and west-central Madagascar.
Habitat: Tropical forests, but seems adaptable to secondary forest, mangroves and even coconut groves.
Food: Fruit, seeds, nectar, other vegetable matter and insect larvae.
Size: 36–44cm (14–17in); 2–3kg (4.4–6.6lb).
Maturity: 3 years.
Breeding: Single young born every 2–3 years.
Life span: 20 years.
Status: Endangered.

Ring-tailed lemur (*Lemur catta*): 38–45cm (15–18in); 2.3–3.5kg (5–8lb)
These lemurs, named after their striking tail markings, spend quite long periods of time on the ground, searching for fallen fruit and other plant material. Although fairly common throughout their range in southern Madagascar, they are declining in number.

Bushbaby (*Galago senegalensis*): 8–21cm (3–8.5in); 95–300g (0.2–0.6lb)
There are three species of bushbaby, or galago, all of which live in Africa. This species is found in open woodland and savannah habitat, from Senegal to Tanzania. It has wide eyes and a long, bushy tail, and is largely nocturnal and tree-dwelling.

Golden potto (*Arctocebus calabarensis*): 23–30cm (9–12in); 266–465g (0.6–1lb)
This little prosimian has long, thick, woolly fur with a golden sheen, and is found in tropical forests from south-eastern Nigeria to southern Congo. This slow-moving solitary animal feeds mostly on insects, and occasionally catches moths in flight.

Potto

Perodicticus potto

These animals forage high up in the treetops at night, climbing slowly through the branches, using their wide, sensitive eyes to locate fruit in the moonlight, and a good sense of smell to find ants and other insects. Pottos also sleep high up in trees during the day.

Females occupy large ranges, big enough to provide food for themselves and their young. Males occupy larger ranges, which cover as many female ranges as possible. Pottos are fairly solitary creatures, but males and females in overlapping ranges make contact throughout the year, communicating with vocal calls and scent marks.

In the first few days of life, baby pottos cling to their mothers' bellies, but later the mothers leave their young hidden near their nests when out foraging. The young are collected at the end of the night. After a few months, the young pottos begin to follow their mothers around as they search for food. The mothers may carry their young on their backs. Young male pottos leave their maternal territories when they are only six months old, but young females stay with their mothers for much longer.

Distribution: Guinea to western Kenya and central Congo.
Habitat: Tropical forest.
Food: Fruit, insects and small vertebrates.
Size: 30–90cm (12–36in); 0.85–1.6kg (1.8–3.5lb).
Maturity: 18 months.
Breeding: Single young, or occasionally twins.
Life span: 25 years.
Status: Common.

When threatened, pottos lower their heads between their forelegs, so that they are protected by their shoulderblades.

RABBITS

There are 54 species of rabbit and hare, all of which belong to the same family, the Leporidae. *They are found in many parts of the world, and some species have been introduced to areas well outside of their original range. Strictly speaking, "hare" is the name given to members of the genus* Lepus, *while all other species in the family are referred to as rabbits.*

Brown hare

Lepus europaeus

Unlike rabbits, hares do not live in burrows. They spend most of the time alone, although a few may be seen together at good feeding sites. Hares are mostly active by night. During the day they crouch in small hollows in the grass called forms, sometimes leaving their backs just visible over the vegetation. In Europe, the main breeding season is in spring, and at this time hares can often be seen during the day, with males fighting one another and pursuing females. Hares fight by kicking with their back legs and boxing with their forelegs.

A number of predators target hares, and in Europe these include foxes and eagles. If a predator detects a hare, the hare flees, running at speeds of up to 60kph (37mph) and making sharp, evasive turns. Injured or captured hares are known to make high-pitched screams.

In order to reduce the risk of losing all of their young leverets to predators, females hide them in different locations in specially dug forms, and visit them one by one to nurse them. Although brown hares are common, changing farming practices have caused a decline in hare numbers in some countries, such as Britain.

Brown hares are easily distinguishable from European rabbits by their larger size and longer ears and limbs.

Distribution: Southern Scandinavia, northern Spain and Britain to Siberia and north-western Iran.
Habitat: Grasslands and agricultural land.
Food: Grass, herbs, crop plants and occasionally twigs and bark.
Size: 60–70cm (24–28in); 3–5kg (6.6–11lb).
Maturity: 1 year.
Breeding: Litter of 1–8 young; 2 or more litters per year.
Life span: 7 years.
Status: Common.

European rabbit

Oryctolagus cuniculus

The rabbit has had a long association with humans, who have prized it for its soft fur and tasty meat. This species was probably introduced to the Mediterranean from its original home in the Iberian Peninsula more than 3,000 years ago. Rabbits often live in large colonies, inhabiting complex labyrinths of burrows, or warrens, that may have hundreds of entrances. Although rabbits live in close proximity to one another, there is a strong dominance hierarchy within a warren. Each male defends a territory, especially during the breeding season.

Rabbits are famed for their rate of reproduction, and a single female has the potential to produce 30 young per year. Rabbits have been introduced to some areas, such as Australia, where there are no predators capable of controlling their numbers. In these places they have created huge problems, crowding out local species and destroying crops. Ironically, rabbit populations in the species' original range in Spain are too small to support their rare predators such as the Iberian lynx and the imperial eagle.

There are as many as 66 domestic breeds of rabbit, and they vary considerably in size, shape and coloration. In Australia, rabbits occurred in such high numbers that they left little food for local marsupials, and even threatened the sheep industry. Two diseases – myxomatosis and viral hemorrhagic – have been successfully introduced into rabbit populations to control them.

Distribution: Originally Iberian Peninsula and southern France. Introduced to most of Europe, north-west Africa, Australia and many other countries.
Habitat: Farmland, grassland and dry shrubland.
Food: Grass, herbaceous plants, bark and twigs.
Size: 35–45cm (14–18in); 1.3–2.3kg (2.8–5lb).
Maturity: 1 year.
Breeding: 1–9 young per litter; up to 7 litters per year.
Life span: 9 years.
Status: Common.

INSECTIVORES

The insectivores are a wide-ranging group of small mammals, all with sensitive and highly mobile noses, small eyes and relatively small brains. They are generally solitary and nocturnal animals, the majority of which eat insects, earthworms and other invertebrates. Their teeth are well designed for eating insects, with long incisors for seizing their prey and sharp molars for dealing with their tough bodies.

Hedgehog

Erinaceus europaeus

Few members of the insectivore family have been able to grow much larger than moles because the food they eat – insects – are so small that they would need to eat a very large quantity. Hedgehogs, however, are more eclectic in their tastes, with a diet that includes earthworms, birds' eggs, frogs, lizards and even snakes. Eating these larger foods has allowed hedgehogs to grow much bigger than is the norm for the group.

Nonetheless, being larger can have its disadvantages, not least being more conspicuous to predators. This is where the hedgehog's most famous asset comes in handy. All over its back the hedgehog has rows of thickened hairs, which narrow at their tips into sharp, prickly points. Using muscles located around the base of the coat, which act like drawstrings, the hedgehog can roll into a ball, becoming an impregnable mass of prickles, which is very effective at deterring the advances of predators.

Distribution: Western Europe and Northern Russia.
Habitat: Woodland, grassland and gardens.
Food: Invertebrates.
Size: 22–28cm (8.8–11in); 0.4–1.2kg (0.9–2.6lb)
Maturity: 2–3 years.
Breeding: 2–6 young born in summer.
Life span: 3–4 years.
Status: Common, but declining in the UK.

The hedgehog's Latin name Erinaceus *is derived from the word ericius, meaning a spiked barrier. Hedgehogs are mostly solitary, but when they do come together, they follow a pecking order.*

Golden mole

Eremitalpa granti

Distribution: South-western Africa.
Habitat: Coastal sand dunes.
Food: Insects, and also small lizards.
Size: 76–87mm (3–3.5in); 120–150g (0.25–0.33lb).
Maturity: Not known.
Breeding: 1 litter of 1–2 young born every year.
Life span: Not known.
Status: Rare.

There are no species of true mole in Africa. Their niche is filled by another group of insectivores called the golden moles. Found mainly in dry sandy areas, golden moles lead entirely subterranean lives, feeding mainly on insects. Their underground existence means that they have little need for vision, and consequently they have lost the power of sight.

Since it is impossible to construct burrows in the dry sands of their desert habitats, golden moles constantly have to plough their way through the sand. Their small but powerful forelimbs are well designed to help them "swim" through sand.

Golden moles may not be able to see, but they do have incredibly acute hearing, being able to pick up the tiny noises made by their insect prey as they move on the surface. By orienting themselves towards these sounds, golden moles can pinpoint the precise location of their prey and emerge from below to snatch their meals.

Skin grows over the golden mole's useless eyes, giving them a bizarre appearance.

Russian desman

Desmana moschata

Distribution: South-western Russia and eastern Europe.
Habitat: Slow rivers and oxbow lakes.
Food: Aquatic invertebrates, including insects, amphibians, crustaceans and molluscs, and also fish and plant roots.
Size: 18–22cm (7–9in); 100–220g (0.2–0.5lb).
Maturity: 1 year.
Breeding: Litters of 1–5 young.
Life span: 2–3 years.
Status: Vulnerable.

Looking somewhat like a cross between a shrew and a mole, there are only two species of desman alive in the world today. The Pyrenean desman lives in northern Spain and Portugal, and its relative the Russian desman inhabits areas in Russia and eastern Europe.

Desmans have webbed feet and broad tails fringed with stiff hairs. These adaptations help them swim, and it is underwater that desmans do most of their hunting, feeling around with their long whiskers for prey items such as dragonfly larvae and tadpoles.

Desmans do not just swim; they also burrow, looking for worms. They tunnel into riverbanks, making networks of burrows which can extend for many metres. The entrances to the systems of tunnels are always located below the waterline, so that the desmans can come and go as they please, without having to worry about any predators that may be watching from above. There are many predators that will feed on desmans, including hawks, kestrels, foxes and weasels.

Like their close relatives the shrews, desmans must feed almost constantly to keep up their energy reserves.

Pygmy white-toothed shrew (*Suncus etruscus*): 3.5–5.2cm (1.5–2in); 1.5–2.5g (0.003–0.005lb)
One of the world's smallest mammals, pygmy white-toothed shrews are found across southern Europe. These shrews have scent glands on their sides, which secrete a pungent odour. The glands are especially well developed in the males during the breeding season, when they are trying to intimidate their rivals and impress females.

Alpine shrew (*Sorex alpinus*): 6–7.5cm (2.5–3in); 5.5–11.5g (0.01–0.025lb)
Inhabiting alpine grasslands up to an altitude of 3,400m (11,333ft) above sea level, alpine shrews are often found in rocky habitats. They are especially common on stony banks and beds of mountain streams, seeking out invertebrate prey. Unlike most shrew species, alpine shrews are adept climbers.

Blind mole (*Talpa caeca*): 9.5–14cm (3.5–5.5in); 65–120g (0.14–0.25lb)
Unlike the common European mole, the blind mole of southern Europe is physically unable to open its eyes. It has membranous coverings over them, which it cannot pull back. However, the membranes do allow some light through, and it is said that blind moles are not totally insensitive to the visual world, being able to react to changes in light and dark.

Rock elephant shrew

Elephantulus myurus

It's not easy being a small diurnal insectivore in the African bush. There is a whole host of other animals that are intent on making them their next meal, from hawks and eagles to small cats, mongooses and a multitude of snakes.

Elephant shrews are well aware of the danger that surrounds them, and they are always on the run from it. They carefully maintain tracks throughout their home ranges, linking feeding areas to bolt holes. These tracks are kept meticulously tidy, and for good reason. The elephant shrews sprint along them at breakneck speed, relying on being simply too fast for their predators to catch them.

Home ranges may be up to 1sq km (0.4sq miles) in size. This is a large area for an animal only 10cm (4in) long to maintain, but where food is scarce, it needs to search a large area to remain well fed. In places where food is much easier to come by, the home ranges tend to be considerably smaller. Young elephant shrews are born very well developed, and after just two days they are able to sprint nimbly around with their mothers.

Elephant shrews get their name from their elongated, mobile snouts.

Distribution: South-eastern Africa.
Habitat: Savannah grassland.
Food: Insects.
Size: 10–14cm (4–5.5in); 40–55g (0.09–0.12lb).
Maturity: 2 months.
Breeding: 1 young per litter.
Life span: 1–3 years.
Status: Common.

SEA MAMMALS

Having conquered the land, some mammals have returned to the seas. Some, such as seals and sea lions, lead predominantly aquatic lives, but must come on to land to give birth. Others have completely dispensed with the terrestrial way of life. The most highly adapted group of sea mammals, comprising whales, porpoises and dolphins, is known as cetaceans. They are highly intelligent.

Mediterranean monk seal

Monachus monachus

Distribution: Less than 20 sites around the Mediterranean and Black Sea and Atlantic coast of Mauritania.
Habitat: Subtropical coastline.
Food: Fish and cephalopods.
Size: 2.3–2.8m (7.5–9.25ft); 250–300kg (550–660lb).
Maturity: 3 years.
Breeding: 1 pup born every other year.
Life span: 24 years.
Status: Critically endangered

This is the darkest seal of the region, uniformly dark brown except for a white patch on the belly.

The Mediterranean monk seal is possibly Europe's most endangered mammal, with only about 500 animals remaining in small, scattered groups around the Mediterranean and Black Sea. There is also a small isolated population off the Atlantic coast of Mauritania, in West Africa.

Monk seals are very intolerant of disturbance. If a pregnant female is distressed, she will abort her foetus, and mothers may desert their young. The increasing development of the Mediterranean and Black Sea coastlines has meant that there are fewer and fewer secluded spots left for these peaceful animals. They also suffer from hunting pressure and from becoming entangled in fishing nets. Being mammals, all seals have to breathe air; if they get caught in fishing nets and held underwater, they drown before too long.

Females give birth to their young in grottoes and sea caves. Those with underwater entrances are particularly favoured. Youngsters stay with their mothers for about three years, learning how to fish and interact with other seals before seeking their own territories.

Harp seal

Pagophilus groenlandicus

Harp seals are very social animals, congregating in huge numbers to give birth on ice floes in areas along the Arctic coastline. However, their sociality has led ultimately to their decline. The pups have very soft, thick fur, which is much sought after in some parts of the world. When the pups are gathered in large numbers, they are easy for hunters to find and club to death. Extensive hunting by humans reduced the total harp seal population from around ten million individuals to just two million by the early 1980s. However, once their plight was realized, hunting pressure was reduced and the population is now slowly recovering.

It will take a long time for harp seal numbers to reach their previous levels because the seals have a low rate of reproduction. Producing just one pup a year means that the population does not grow very quickly. When hunting, adult seals may dive to depths of 200m (666ft) in search of herring and cod, which make up the bulk of their diet.

The luxuriant fur of harp seal pups keeps them warm as they grow up on the Arctic icepack.

Distribution: Arctic Ocean.
Habitat: Open sea for most of the year.
Food: Pelagic crustaceans and fish.
Size: 1.7–1.9m (5.5–6ft); 120–130kg (260–285lb).
Maturity: 5 years.
Breeding: 1 pup born every year.
Life span: 16–30 years.
Status: Vulnerable.

Narwhal

Monodon monoceros

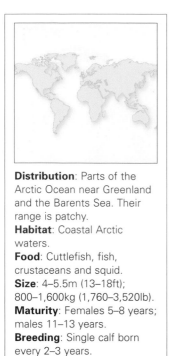

Distribution: Parts of the Arctic Ocean near Greenland and the Barents Sea. Their range is patchy.
Habitat: Coastal Arctic waters.
Food: Cuttlefish, fish, crustaceans and squid.
Size: 4–5.5m (13–18ft); 800–1,600kg (1,760–3,520lb).
Maturity: Females 5–8 years; males 11–13 years.
Breeding: Single calf born every 2–3 years.
Life span: 50 years.
Status: Common.

Some people believe that the bizarre appearance of the narwhal first gave rise to the legend of the unicorn. The function of the male's long tusk is not properly known, but it may function as a hunting implement, or as a tool to break up ice and allow access to the air, so that the animals can breathe. However, the most favoured explanation is that the males joust with each other, fighting over access to females during the breeding season.

The narwhal's swollen forehead is known as its melon, a feature shared with other toothed whales, such as dolphins. The melon serves to focus the ultrasonic clicks that narwhals use, like other small cetaceans, to navigate and find their food. As in a sophisticated sonar system, narwhals listen as the high-frequency sounds they make rebound off objects nearby. So sensitive is this method of orientation that narwhals are able not only to tell what is food and what is not, but also how big, how distant and how quickly a potential prey item is moving.

The male narwhal's tusk is in fact an elongated front tooth that spirals as it grows from a hole in its lips. Females may possess a short tusk, too. Their name means "corpse whale" in Old Norse, perhaps referring to their bluish-grey skin with white blotches.

Atlantic humpback dolphin

Sousa teuszii

The humpback dolphin gets its name from its distinctive method of surfacing and its slightly bulbous dorsal fin.

Distribution: Eastern Atlantic Ocean off West Africa.
Habitat: Tropical coastal waters, usually less than 20m (65ft) deep, and tidal zones of rivers.
Food: Fish.
Size: 1.2–2.5m (4–8.25ft); 75–150kg (165–330lb).
Maturity: Between 4 and 8 years.
Breeding: Single calf born every 1–2 years.
Life span: Not known.
Status: Declining because of habitat loss and entanglement in fishing nets.

Atlantic humpbacks are shy dolphins and rarely approach boats, making them a difficult species for scientists to observe and study. Political instability in many West African countries along the coasts of which this dolphin lives has also compounded the problems of studying these animals.

They inhabit tropical coastal waters, preferring to stay in water no deeper than 20m (65ft) and with shallow banks. They also like river channels and muddied waters. Typical school sizes range from between three and seven individuals, but groups of up to 25 have been observed. As these dolphins get older, they become more and more solitary by nature, and eventually hardly ever associate with other individuals.

The humpback dolphin has a unique way of surfacing: the beak and often the entire head break the surface of the water before the body arches tightly, making the hump and dorsal fin more prominent. Orcas (killer whales) are a major threat to this species. They locate the dolphins by listening in to their echolocation calls. By staying close to land, the dolphins are able to disrupt their calls and thwart these aggressors.

White-beaked dolphin

Lagenorhynchus albirostris

Distribution: Ranges widely through the North Atlantic and Arctic Oceans.
Habitat: Coastal waters.
Food: Medium-sized fish, squid and crustaceans form the bulk of the diet.
Size: 2.3–2.8m (7.5–9.25ft); 180kg (396lb).
Maturity: Not known.
Breeding: 1 calf born every year.
Life span: Not known.
Status: Common.

Dolphins are notoriously difficult animals to study because they are relatively small, and also very wide-ranging. Consequently, not much is known about the habits of this remarkable group compared to most land-living mammals.

Like most cetaceans, white-beaked dolphins live in groups known as schools, which have very complex social structures. Schools are usually made up of 2–20 individuals, but occasionally lots of schools will come together to form large aggregations containing more than 1,000 individuals.

Dolphins are famed for a behaviour known as breaching, when they leap clear of the water, somersault and splash back down through the waves. Dolphins have also been observed playing games underwater, such as "chase the seaweed". White-beaked dolphins undertake annual migrations, moving between temperate and subpolar waters, tracking their favoured prey of mackerel and herring.

The white-beaked dolphin's counter-shaded coloration, with a darker upperside and pale belly, helps to camouflage it from both above and below.

Harbour porpoise (*Phocoena phocoena*): 1.3–1.9m (4.25–6ft); 35–90kg (77–198lb)
Generally found in small groups in shallow coastal waters and river estuaries, harbour porpoises are relatively common in European waters. These social, highly vocal cetaceans live in groups of up to 15 members. Porpoises generally are distinguished from dolphins by having blunt faces that lack "beaks".

False killer whale (*Pseudorca crassidens*): 3.7–5.5m (12.25–18ft); 1.2–2 tonnes (2,640–4,400lb)
Like its namesake the killer whale, the false killer whale is actually a member of the dolphin family. This is a wide-ranging species, which travels throughout the world's oceans. The false killer whale is able to reach speeds of up to 30 knots (30 nautical mph or 55kph) and is often encountered racing ships.

Common seal

Phoca vitulina

One of the two seal species found commonly in British waters, the common seal has a dog-like face. Its snout is much more rounded than the Roman-style nose which typifies the grey seal, Britain's other common seal.

It is difficult to get a good estimate of the common seal's population size because it lives in small, widely distributed groups, and is highly mobile.

Common seals have large, sensitive eyes with specialized retinas, which allow them to see well underwater. However, sometimes the water is too murky for seals to be able to hunt by sight. At these times common seals switch to another sense – touch. Their long whiskers are highly sensitive and allow the seals to feel for prey in the gloom.

Distribution: North Atlantic, Pacific and Arctic coastlines.
Habitat: Sheltered coastal waters.
Food: Fish, cephalopods and crustaceans.
Size: 1.2–2m (4–6.5ft); 45–130kg (99–285lb).
Maturity: Females 2 years; males 5 years.
Breeding: Single pup produced every year.
Life span: 26–32 years.
Status: Common.

From a distance, a seal's head poking above the waves can closely resemble that of a human. They are sometimes mistaken for swimmers in trouble. The common seal is also known as the harbour seal.

INDEX

ACKNOWLEDGEMENTS
The publisher would like
to thank the following for
permission to reproduce their
photographs in this book.

Key: l=left, r=right, t=top,
m=middle, b=bottom

NHPA: 8bl, 16tr, 16b, 18t, 18b,
19t, 21t, 21br, 24t, 26t, 26b, 27tl,
28t, 30t, 31t, 31b.
Tim Ellerby: 31m.